How to Help Your Teenager
POSTPONE
SEXUAL
INVOLVEMENT

How to Help Your Teenager

POSTPONE
SEXUAL
INVOLVEMENT

Marion Howard

Continuum | *New York*

**To my daughter Katherine,
from whom I have learned so much**

1988

The Continuum Publishing Company
370 Lexington Avenue
New York, NY 10017

Printed in the United States of America

Library of Congress Cataloging-in-Publication Data

Howard, Marion, 1936–
    How to help your teenager postpone sexual involvement / Marion
Howard.
    p.   cm.
    ISBN 0-8264-0412-X
    1. Sexual ethics. 2. Teenagers—Sexual behavior. 3. Parenting.
I. Title.
HQ32.H69   1988   88-11940
649′.65—dc19   CIP

Contents

78331

Preface

This book is written to give parents tools to help young teens bridge the gap between their physical development and their cognitive ability to handle the implications of such development. Surveys of adolescents have indicated that many young people do not want to become sexually involved but are pressured into doing so.

Young teens are confronted with sexual feelings, including a need for closeness and affection. They search for ways to handle these feelings. Often they are unsure about how to handle situations in which there may be curiosity but no meaningful love relationship. In relationships with deeper feelings, they search for ways to handle aroused sexual feelings.

Parents have an appropriate role to play in helping their teens in this area. This book is intended to give parents insights into the ways in which adolescent sexual decision-making is influenced by various stages of adolescent growth and development. It is also aimed at increasing parents' understanding of the social and peer pressures young people experience with respect to sexual behavior. Finally, it is aimed at increasing the skill of parents in communicating with their teens about postponing sexual involvement.

I wish to thank Marie Mitchell, R.N., for her collaboration on programs aimed at helping young people postpone sexual involvement as well as those designed to help parents support young teens in this area. Her insights and hard work have made such programs as "Postponing Sexual Involvement: An Educational Series for Young People," "Postponing Sexual Involvement: An Educational Program for Parents," and "Making Responsible Decisions" possible. Much of the material in this book has been taken from such collaborative efforts.

Introduction

Today in the United States, 45 percent of all sixteen-year-olds have had sexual intercourse, 33 percent of all fifteen-year-olds. Faced with such facts, parents wonder what they can do to help their child postpone sexual involvement. They also wonder what has brought about such a dramatic change in our society. The answers are not simple. However, armed with certain information, parents can enhance their child's ability to manage his or her sexuality during adolescence.

Earlier Fertility

One hundred years ago, young people in the United States began puberty around the ages of seventeen or eighteen. Fertility thus came at a time when young people generally had developed some job skills and often had worked for a while. It also came close to an age that was considered appropriate for marriage. When young people married and began having children, there was often an extensive family to help them. However, the timing of puberty has been changing. The age at first menstruation—the outward sign in girls that they have become fertile—has been dropping three months every ten years during the last century. This change is thought to be due to better nutrition and health care.

Today the average age of becoming fertile for girls is twelve years and five months. Some girls, in fact, start having their menstrual periods as early as nine years of age and others as late as sixteen. Once a girl begins having periods, even at age nine, she can become pregnant if she has sexual intercourse. She can also become pregnant *before* she starts having periods, if the very first egg cell she releases is fertilized. The average age of beginning fertility for boys (the first emission of sperm is the outward sign that boys have become fertile) is thirteen years and five months. Boys may become fertile as early as age ten or as late as age seventeen.

The Impact of Early Fertility

Early fertility, however, is inconsistent with other requirements of society. Because of the increased demands of a technological world, most young people face many years of schooling following puberty before they can develop the job skills our society requires. Meaningful employment leading to well-paid careers is something they enter into only after completion of high school and further education or training. Most adults feel that marriage and childbearing should wait until young people have completed their education and training and worked for a time. For many young people, that means they will be in their twenties.

This lowering of the age of fertility, combined with changes in societal expectations with respect to young people, places a whole new framework around adolescent sexuality. Rather than the natural onset of the capacity for fertilization and conception being followed soon by marriage and childbearing and child rearing, we have a set of circumstances under which fertility is better followed by a long delay before family life is established. This creates dilemmas for parents, for society, and for young people themselves. It also creates problems for the health professionals whose job it is to help young people protect their fertility so that they can bear healthy children at the time they choose to do so.

Risks of Early Sexual Involvement

Obstetricians and gynecologists agree that the best way for young people to protect their ability to conceive and bear a child or to father a child is to begin to have sexual intercourse as close to the time they wish to begin having children as possible. Infections developed as a consequence of earlier sexual intercourse can affect the capacity for impregnation, conception, and childbearing as well as injure the health of the infant.

In the United States today, infertility (the inability to have a baby) is increasing, particularly among young women. Between the 1970s and 1980s, infertility nearly doubled among young white women and nearly tripled among young black women. Primarily this rise in infertility is thought to be due to infections contracted by young women beginning sexual intercourse at young ages. Because they started so young, over time such young women were more likely to have a greater number of sexual partners than in the past. Increased incidences of pelvic inflammatory disease and cervical cancer have been reported. Sometimes young women show no symptoms of infection and, if undiagnosed and untreated, the infection can progress to a point where their reproductive systems are damaged. Young men also can damage their fathering capacity and render themselves infertile. Young people who contract sexually transmitted infections need to seek a cure immediately.

However, some diseases spread by having sexual intercourse cannot be cured. Herpes, for example, is a painful sexually transmitted infection for which there is no remedy. In addition to bearing the hardship of the disease, the person having it must take responsibility for telling anyone with whom he or she wants to become sexually involved about the disease, and must share in protecting that other person from the disease. Babies born to women with herpes sores in the birth canal can contract the disease.

AIDS is a very serious disease, spread in large measure by sexual contact. Thus far, over half of those who have been infected with the AIDS virus have developed the AIDS disease. The AIDS disease leads to early death. Currently there is no cure. Children born to those who have the AIDS virus often are doomed to short and painful lives. Once people are infected with the virus, it never leaves their body. It robs the body of its natural ability to fight off disease and prevents the body from getting well. One cannot tell by looking at a person if they have the AIDS virus. It takes from two to five years for signs of AIDS to show. Some people never show signs.

Having sex with many people—or even having sex with just one person, if he or she is a person who has the AIDS virus or could have had sex with anyone who carried it— increases the risk of getting AIDS. It is unlikely that those who begin having sex at young ages will be able to keep just one sexual partner until they are in their twenties and ready for the responsibilities of marriage and child rearing. Their risk of contracting an infection such as AIDS therefore increases.

Pregnancy at a young age poses other problems. The younger the girl, the greater the likelihood she will have health problems during pregnancy and/or give birth to a baby who will have health problems. Babies born to young girls are more likely to be born too soon and be of low birth weight. Such babies may have lifelong handicapping conditions, such as mental retardation. Girls who give birth at young ages are four times as likely to die in childbirth as are women who give birth in their twenties.

Thus, the risk of pregnancy and parenting at a young age, the harmful effects of sexually transmitted infections, and the need for the protection of fertility all underscore why parents should be concerned about the sexual involvement of teen-agers. However, even if these risks could be eliminated, there are many other concerns that parents generally have about the sexual involvement of their adolescent.

Other Concerns About Early Sexual Involvement

For example, the technological advances with respect to methods of contraceptives, although potentially helpful to young people, cause some parental concern. One reason for this is that, because birth control means that conception no longer need be a natural consequence of sexual intercourse, much of the attention given sexual intercourse as the precursor of pregnancy has been supplanted with attention given to sexual intercourse as the source of immense pleasure.

Although the pleasure aspect of sexual contact has always been acknowledged, it was previously tied to potential childbearing. To a large extent, the concept of *pro*creation has been replaced by a concept of *re*creation. In light of the earlier ages at puberty, this notion of sexual pleasure independent of the old context of family and childbearing creates new behavioral dilemmas for parents, society, and young people themselves. When asked why they think teens have sex, young people often put "fun" as one of the key reasons.

Parents worry that engaging in sex solely for fun will lead to the adolescent's never moving beyond superficial, purely physical sexual relationships. Parents most often want their children to grow to an adulthood in which they are capable of having meaningful, intimate relationships that include a satisfying sexual life. In particular, parents are concerned that early sexual involvement on the part of their adolescent may include experiences that will detract from that possibility.

For example, there are issues of trust and confidentiality that young people may not be able to handle. The result can be hurt feelings or lowered self-esteem. Young people often form opinions about which behaviors are going to be successful for them in life and which are not; new patterns of how to treat people of the opposite sex are being learned. Situations that lack mutual respect and caring may end with one or both young people feeling "used." They can also end with one person feeling that it is all right to use someone sexually in order to get what they want.

Often, becoming involved in a sexual relationship means that young people spend less time in other important areas. The sexual part of the relationship can come to dominate, so that the couple do not take time to get to know each other in more important ways. They can be distracted from their studies, have less interest in sports and other extra-curricular activities, as well as put reduced time and effort into getting to know their peers. Further, mutual suspicions and jealousies surrounding sexual behavior can interfere with learning more about the wide variety of positive relationships that can exist between people. For example, young people need to know it is possible to have a meaningful, even an intimate, relationship with someone without becoming sexually involved.

Parents also generally want their adolescent to experience the beauty and joy of sex within a lasting relationship—one uncluttered with fear of discovery, hurried behavior, anxiety or guilt. They are not sure that that is achievable during the adolescent years.

Parents are aware that there are many responsibilities that go along with a sexual relationship for which young people are not ready. They understand that adolescents have a difficult time accepting full responsibility for the consistent use of birth control. They know that adolescents are not mature enough to accept complete responsibility for the consequences of their actions. For example, should a pregnancy occur, adolescents are not yet old enough to provide a stable home for a child and support and nurture it.

Many parents have strong religious beliefs and feel sexual intercourse on the part of their adolescent would violate those beliefs in a devastating way. They feel that the young person would soon regret his or her choice and that the accompanying guilt and loss of self-respect would be harmful to the child in both a religious and social context.

Puberty Affects Both Parent and Adolescent

As their children enter puberty, parents experience new feelings and attitudes triggered by the changes their child is experiencing. As the child continues to mature, and parents sense that the adolescent has become sexually curious and may be beginning sexual exploration, a new reality emerges. Some parents, who have never talked with their children about sexuality, feel anxiety or concern and a need to do something. As young people begin to date, additional urgency is often added to these feelings. Parents may not know how to communicate their concerns to their adolescent in ways that will be helpful to the young person.

Even parents who may have talked rather freely with their children over the years, answering their questions carefully and honestly, may start feeling new anxiety or concern. They may not know what else to share with their child. It is one thing to tell a child about how the baby grows inside the mother's body or how the father provides the sperm that meets with the mother's egg, and another thing to know what to say to a boy experiencing frequent erections and thinking about how much he would like to have sex with his girlfriend. It is easy to encourage a daughter to be attractive to the opposite sex, but then difficult to know what to say when her boyfriend becomes the most important person in the world to her and she spends every single minute she can with him. And it may appear reasonable to assume that twelve-year-olds are just having fun with their pals until it is discovered that they have been gathering at parent-absent homes with opportunities for smoking, drinking, and sexual experimentation.

Some parents, because they don't know what to do, end up doing nothing. Other parents may become involved in giving lectures to their adolescent that do not make either parent or adolescent feel like much has been accomplished. Threats, warnings—all well intentioned—may have similar poor results. Some parents inappropriately clamp down on where their children can go and what they can do, without real consideration of mutually agreeable ways of limiting the opportunities for sexual involvement.

Other parents focus on nonsexual aspects of the child's life and convince themselves that sex is something their adolescent has no interest in. Parents often misjudge the age at which their child is thinking about sex or experimenting with sex. Parents will say, "My son just isn't interested in that yet"; "My daughter is still naive"; or, "My child would never do anything like that." Because they convince themselves their adolescent has no interest in sex, sexual intercourse is judged as something their child could never or would never become involved in. In this way they avoid confronting themselves with the needs and feelings young people have.

Some parents acknowledge their child's interest in sex but abdicate responsibility for their child's sexual behavior by just hoping their adolescent will not *do* anything. Some even hope that if their adolescent does become sexually involved, they won't find out, because such knowledge would pose more problems for them than they feel they know how to handle.

Parents sometimes seem to feel that if they ignore their child's emerging sexuality and the concomitant need for support and guidance, that need will go away. Still other parents acknowledge that their adolescent has needs in the area of learning to manage his/her sexuality but confess to feeling that they wish someone else would talk with their adolescent. Still others feel their adolescent somehow will muddle through, just as they did.

Parental Insecurity About Changes

A great many of these attitudes and actions stem from parental beliefs that they do not know how to handle their adolescent as a sexual human being. There are some very understandable reasons for this.

Parents are aware that much of the world today has changed with respect to sexuality from the time in which they grew up, but they are not exactly sure how that applies to their child. Does the changed world make what their young person is experiencing and feeling very different from what they may have experienced or felt at similar ages? Although parents may believe that it is their duty to educate their child in matters of human sexuality, they often have concerns about how effective the education they give will be in light of the changes in the world today. For example, the importance of the peer group has increased; and sexual acts are commonly shown in the media.

Because they were raised in a different era, parents may have no role models for how to talk to their child about sexuality. When parents are asked, "What messages did you receive from your parents about sexuality?" their answers often are: "My parents never said anything"; "My parents conveyed that it was dirty"; "My parents told me nice girls didn't do that"; "My parents just said, 'Don't get a girl in trouble' "; "They just gave me a book to read." Therefore, it is difficult for these parents to know how to approach the subject with their children, what to cover, and how to cover it. No one did it for them, so they are not sure how to go about it with their children.

Another concern parents often have is the changing knowledge in the area of human sexuality. Even though for years they themselves have sexually related to a person of the opposite sex and have had children, often parents do not know the correct names of the various parts of the reproductive system and exactly how the system functions. Increasing technology, such as that with respect to the wide variety of birth-control methods, or changing information such as that related to sexually transmitted infections may make some parents fear they don't have enough information to talk with their adolescent and/or answer their child's questions. Some parents believe that if they talk to their adolescent about human sexuality it will encourage the youth to be more curious and want to experiment. They are reluctant to tell the adolescent about birth control, thinking it somehow will imply that they are condoning sexual intercourse among young people or even giving young people permission to become sexually involved.

Finally, some parents are embarrassed because to them sexual intercourse is a private behavior. They may have tried to conceal from their children the fact that they were having sexual intercourse, and even may feel that they have been successful at hiding this behavior. Talking to their adolescent about sexuality means that they may have to acknowledge that they have had intercourse and are still having intercourse. They may be afraid of how their adolescent will think about them and that behavior. They may be afraid their adolescent will ask them personal questions about sexual intercourse: how it is for them, how many times they have it, when they first had it. Or they may be afraid their adolescent will ask them questions about other people's sexual behaviors that they feel are offensive or have little understanding or knowledge about.

The Parental Role and Its Importance

It is most vital, however, that parents recognize how important a resource they are for their young person. Since the child's birth they have been helping shape his or her values, attitudes, and behaviors. All along, their sexual attitudes and feelings have been conveyed to their offspring whether they have ever spoken of it or not. For example, how parents have reacted to sexual scenes shown on television or sexual stories read about in the news has helped shape their child's impressions of sexuality. How parents have treated each other and related to each other has helped shape the child's ideas of male–female relationships.

The onset of puberty and the ensuing developmental years means that parents have an even greater opportunity to influence their child's sexual values, attitudes, and behaviors because these are the years in which sexuality begins to take on more concrete meaning for the young person. Parents must become involved in this area as transmitters of their culture and because of their obligation to society and themselves to produce a new, sexually responsible generation.

It is important for parents to realize that, in today's sexual environment, leaving children to "muddle through" about the appropriateness of their sexual feelings and behaviors will not work very well. Young people need help. The electronic media has brought sexual behavior right into our homes. Adolescents regularly view people on TV or in the movies who are in bed making love. The great variety of sexual life-styles and behaviors of both the public and private individuals is also made very apparent to young people by TV, radio, and newspapers. Such behaviors often are confusing or misleading to young people. Peer pressures toward sexual involvement can be even more difficult for young people to handle.

It is clear that social and peer pressures toward early sexual involvement today often propel young people into behaviors they really don't want to engage in. Parents must play a strong role in helping young people sort through the various images and messages they receive so that they can develop the skills and abilities to resist becoming sexually involved before they are ready for such involvement.

In order to do this, parents must talk to and with their children. Part of these discussions will involve reinforcing values, religious beliefs, and making clear family expectations. Another part will be giving facts needed to understand human sexuality and provide a basis for intelligent decision-making. Another part will be providing behavioral guidance and establishing supervisory guidelines. Another part will be teaching their young person skills that will enable them to better handle social and peer pressures.

By communicating with their children about sex, parents can build in their offspring a strong sense of respect for their body, its reproductive capacity, and its responsible use. They can also provide the support young people need to manage their sexuality in a changed society. Finally, they can help young people postpone sexual involvement until such time as they are older and more clearly able to see for themselves the implications of such behavior on their future.

1

How Adolescent Growth and Development Affect Sexual Decision-Making

Despite the fact that the age at which young people become fertile has been getting earlier, ages of other important developmental areas do not appear to be lowering at a similar pace. The completion of mental, psychosocial, and moral growth and development occurs several years after the onset of fertility. Young people are at a real disadvantage, therefore, when forced to cope with social and peer pressures related to their sexual maturity.

Cognitive Development and Its Effect on Decision-Making

For example, it is not normal for pubescent young people to think like adults. In many ways their thinking process is more circumscribed than that of adults. Beginning around age eleven, adolescents begin developing new capabilities that eventually allow them to think in different ways. Somewhere around age sixteen most young people have acquired these new, more adult, thinking skills. Until this process is complete, however, adolescents tend to think about things in much more concrete ways than do adults. Even after this important change in thinking has taken place, it may take one or two years more to integrate the changes into actual control of behavior.

As a consequence of their concrete thinking, adolescents tend to focus on the present. The immediate experience is what is most real to them. Adolescents in this concrete stage of thinking are concerned with their world as it is today, not what it might be like in the future. If adolescents in the eighth grade are thinking ahead, it is most likely about what they are going to do on the weekend. If they are more farsighted, they may be wondering if they are going to make it through the eighth grade. They are not generally thinking about their life five years from now.

Adolescents who are concrete thinkers are much less likely to see the cause-and-effect aspect of behavior. It is much more difficult for them to be planners because the abstract quality of adult thinking is not yet fully developed. Without the ability to plan—which requires not only the ability to think about tomorrow but the ways in which today's actions could lead to consequences tomorrow—adolescent decision-making differs considerably from that of adults. This can make sexual decision-making a particular problem for adolescents because of the potential long-range consequences of sexual behavior.

Although most adolescents know that sex can lead to a pregnancy, they often focus on more immediate feelings. "The other guys will think I'm cool if they know I've had sex." "Maybe if I have sex with my boyfriend, it will keep him interested in me." At best they think, "I hope I don't get pregnant" (or "I hope I don't get her pregnant"). However, pregnancy is seen only as an immediate problem. They do not think of the ways it could impact on their future. They do not understand in a realistic way that at the end of nine months of a pregnancy, they will have a baby. They cannot conceptualize the next eighteen years of their life, so they cannot begin to imagine what it would mean to have full responsibility for another human being during that time.

Even more immediate events are not clear to them. They cannot conceptualize that a pregnancy means they will have to decide whether or not to keep the baby and how difficult a decision that will be. They do not think about notions such as, if they keep the baby, they will have to resolve where the baby will sleep, how they will get funds to meet the expenses of the baby, who will care for the child so they can meet their own basic needs or wants: school, social activities, and so forth. Unfortunately, young people cannot conceptualize what the impact of early childbearing might be on their later life: that, for example, at age twenty-one they might be a single parent who has never finished school and has no marketable job skills.

Sexual intercourse is more related to "How I feel about this person right now," not "How will I feel about this person next week, next year, three years from now?" They cannot grasp the connection between how a sexual experience might affect their self-image several months or a year from now, after the relationship has ended. They cannot perceive that, later on, the sexual experience might negatively color their relationship with another person who could be far more important to them than the person they are choosing to have sex with now.

Application of Thinking Skills

Indeed, that is one reason why the use of contraception is often difficult for young people: it, too, requires thinking about the future. It requires connecting sexual intercourse with possible problems—pregnancy or sexually transmitted infection—and then linking all the events that might follow from such an occurrence. For example (both herpes and AIDS are currently incurable.) In this instance imagining what it would be like to go through life with an incurable contagious disease is required, and in the case of AIDS imagining what it would be like to die from the disease.

Second, it requires planning: consideration of the safe sexual history of the other person, knowing in advance the time when one is going to have sexual intercourse so that a method of protection can be obtained, and then making sure the method is used prior to having sex.

Adults can associate all the things involved—assessment of the sexual history, organizing time, getting money, making the trip to obtain a protective contraceptive method, planning to have it available when needed—with the end goal of avoiding negative long-range consequences. Adults also have an enormous advantage in that they can associate all the things involved in avoiding sexual intercourse as part of a caring relationship as well. Such associations are much more difficult for adolescents—almost impossible for many.

That is also why some adolescents view and use abortion as a method of birth control. Because they are not as planful as adults, they do not take the steps necessary to prevent pregnancy. Therefore, they are left with making choices *after* conception rather than before it. They fail to see in advance the full implications of having to make a choice about abortion. They do not conceptualize how much more difficult the reality of that choice and that action will be in contrast to their imagined version of abortion as an easy solution to an unplanned pregnancy.

Thus, when a parent says to a teen, "You ought not to have sex because you might get pregnant" (or "You might cause a pregnancy"), the adult may have a whole series of conceptualizations associated with that statement that do not exist for the adolescent. All the adolescent hears and understands is that there might be a pregnancy. For some, that may seem not like such a terrible problem. However, even if they see pregnancy as a problem, it is usually seen only as an immediate one.

Parents therefore need to be very clear in their statements. Parents of a daughter might have to give concrete information, such as: "You ought not to have sex, because you might get pregnant. If you get pregnant, that means you will have a baby growing inside you for nine months. A lot of things in your life will change. Your body shape will change, you won't be able to wear the clothes you have, you might not fit into your regular seat at school and have to sit elsewhere. At the end of nine months of being pregnant, it means you will give birth to a baby.

"Keeping the baby and trying to be a parent would mean that you would have to figure out how to have the baby cared for, so you could go back to school. Having a child to care for over the next eighteen years will mean that you will not be free to come and go with friends, as others your age will be. Any further education you get or what job you take will be limited by the amount of child care you can get, how much it will cost you, and whether or not it is available close to where you need it."

This taking of young people mentally through the adult associative process may be very necessary to help them better understand how their sexual behavior could dramatically change the circumstances of their lives. Although the immediate changes a parent describes will be much easier for a young teen to grasp and much more significant to them than the longer-term aspects, one goal a parent should have is to help the young person form some linkage between acts in the present and consequences beyond the immediate.

Many young men, for example, do not know that if a woman receives public assistance for the care of the child, the baby's father is incurring every penny she receives as a debt that he must pay back to the state. Even if the young man is in school, he has a financial obligation to pay for the child's care. The only way he can avoid accumulating a debt for all the support payments the mother of his child receives from the state is to make whatever regular support payments the state determines he can afford even while he is in school.

Thus, a parent might convey to a boy, "You ought not to have sex at your age because you might get a girl pregnant. If she is pregnant, she will have a baby growing inside her for nine months. During those nine months her shape will change. She won't be able to wear the clothes she has now. She will not be able to hide from people the fact that she is going to have a baby. Your relationships with a lot of people may change. Your teachers and coaches may feel differently about you. Certainly the girl and her parents will feel differently about you.

"At the end of the nine months, she will give birth to a baby. She will decide whether or not she wants to keep the baby. You have no legal right over that decision. If she decides to keep the baby, however, you will have a financial responsibility until the child is even older than you are now. If you cannot pay all the costs of the child's care, and welfare help is needed, all the money paid for the care of the child by welfare will have to be paid back by you to the state when you have a job and can do that. The state can even get whoever you work for to take some of the money you owe out of your pay every week.

"The responsibility for the baby could prevent you from doing many things you want to do—you may not have time for sports if you have to get a job while you are in school to help support the baby. After you finish high school, you may not be able to go to college, travel, get the car you want, or go and do what your friends are doing if you have the responsibilities of a baby and its expenses. The obligation for the child will continue until the child becomes an adult. That means you will have that financial responsibility till you are middle-aged."

Or the parent may say, for example, "Sometimes people

get into situations where there are no good choices, just choices. You make your decision and live with it for the rest of your life. If the girl has an abortion, there is one set of consequences. If the girl keeps the baby, there is another set of consequences. Even if the girl places the baby in adoption, there are consequences. For example, I have known where you are every day of your life, and that has been important to me. You could spend a lot of time wondering where your child was and how life was going for him or her. And you might spend a lot of time feeling guilty that you aren't taking care of your child or wishing that life had been different."

Some young people may respond with the notion that if the girl gets an abortion there won't be any consequences. It may be necessary for the parent to reemphasize that in adolescence pregnancy is usually a situation with no good solutions, just choices and having to live with whatever consequences flow from making a particular choice. In addition, the parent may want to point out that it is impossible to know in advance exactly what feelings a person will have when faced with the choice of abortion.

Some young people who think abortion will be a viable option for them may find they actually cannot go through it when the time comes. Or sometimes it turns out that only one of the people responsible for the pregnancy favors abortion, while the other doesn't want it used as a solution. A young person who feels positively about abortion may proceed with that action and then find he or she has regrets or continued bad feelings about it. Although this does not always happen, the important point parents need to share with adolescents is that it is impossible to know in advance of the situation how it will work out. Therefore, abortion is not a simple solution.

Having to make a decision about abortion, just as having to make a choice about adoption, or having to make a choice about trying to parent at a young age, can be prevented. No young person should put themselves in that situation. It is also important to point out that having to make such choices can irrevocably change the relationship between the two people involved. Feelings and lives are generally not the same, whatever course of action is chosen.

Young people must be helped to see that all actions have consequences. Risking unwanted, unplanned, or premature pregnancy will mean uncomfortable choices and potential long-range impact on the lives of those involved. Parents can help young people understand how much better and easier it is for a couple to communicate to each other that they want to avoid pregnancy and make decisions about how to achieve that than later on having to discuss and make the difficult and emotional choices surrounding abortion, adoption, or lifetime parenting responsibilities.

Some young people may be very strongly attached to one another and feel that, if a pregnancy occurs, they will resolve it by marrying one another. Often young people have a very limited notion of the degree of commitment marriage requires and the amount of compromise, problem-solving, and hard work that is needed to make a marriage succeed. Parents will need to point out that more than one out of every two marriages among young people ends in divorce within the first five years. Young people are still growing and changing, and, until they have resolved developmental issues and had a chance to find out who they are, it is difficult for them to select the type of person with whom they can develop a long-term committed relationship. Even more difficult is having the *ability* to carry out such a commitment at a young age. Marriages that are forced because of circumstances also run the chance of having that become the rationale for separation when the going gets rough. Furthermore, the endless pressures of child-rearing responsibilities at a young age can weaken a relationship rather than make it stronger.

Helping Young Teens Understand Consequences

Another way to convey information to adolescents is in the form of a guided discussion using some questions. It is important to think about the way to try to help young people link acts in the present to consequences in the future. Youth often resist information presented in lecture form. Thus, a parent might offer, "Teenage pregnancy is a real problem for kids today and I want to make sure you've had a chance to think it through, so you don't get caught.

"What in your life do you think might change if you were involved in a teenage pregnancy?" (Response.) "Yes, that's true. I was also thinking it might change . . ." (Add an example you think important.)

"Let's see, if you became a parent now, how old would you be when the child became an adult?" (Response.) "What things do you expect to have done by the time you are age . . . .?" (Response: "Finished school," Gotten a job," "Gotten married," "Got an apartment," "Gotten a car," etc.) "How might having a child now affect those things you expect to do by the time you are age . . . ?" (Response.) "Yes, that's true. I was also thinking it might affect . . ." (Add an example you think important but was overlooked.) "What are the ways you've thought about to keep from getting involved in a teen pregnancy?"

Sometimes young people know other young people who are teen parents. In some cases, such young people can serve as dramatic examples of how becoming a parent at a young age can impact on a young person's life. In other cases, the changes may not be readily apparent. The girl who had a baby may still come to school, may still have some time with her friends.

Because of their concrete thinking stage, it may be difficult for young people to see the ways in which the young mother's life is different from theirs. They do not imagine that when the young mother goes home she is never free. The responsibility for the baby is always there. They cannot think ahead to see how the baby will continue to impact on the young person's life; for example, how the baby will influence when the time comes for moving out on one's own, how any money earned will be spent. They don't understand what the additional strain of providing constant care and guidance for another person's life might be on both the mental and physical health of the young parent.

It is important for adults to point out these examples to young people. "I'm glad Jeanette is able to continue school even though she has the responsibility of the baby. When she gets home, however, I am sure her life is very different from yours. You have time to sit and watch TV or lounge in your room. You don't have to hurry your bath and you can spend time on the telephone. She has to care for her baby whether she feels like it or not. If she wants to sleep and the baby doesn't, she has to care for it—even if it's in the middle of the night. She can't go out unless she can find someone to care for the baby. She has to take care of that baby seven days a week—there are no vacations when you have a baby. And caring for the baby will go on for years and years."

Other Limits on Thinking

Another aspect of the abstract thinking that adults use enables them to understand risks or probability in a way different from young people. Young people need to know that girls who give birth to a baby while still very young are more likely to die in childbirth. The child of a young girl is more likely to be born before it is ready to be born and not weigh as much as it should. This can be very serious for the baby, and the baby can be mentally retarded or have other lifelong handicapping conditions because of it. A mentally retarded baby will be a child who will need very patient parents who are willing and able to give it special amounts of care and attention. Therefore, it is very important that young girls *wait* to become pregnant in order to increase their chances of having a healthy baby.

Even when given such information, however, the girl still may not be able to apply it. Instead, she may think, "My friend had a baby and there was nothing wrong with her or her baby." The concrete thinking stage often makes what their limited experience has taught them seem more real to young people than any statistical likelihood of occurrences.

Parents are used to using probability. They know, for example, that if their child does not wear a seatbelt in a car, there is increased likelihood of serious injury in an accident, so they have probably made their children wear seatbelts. They know, also, that if they approach a train track and see a train coming, there is a probability they might not make it across in time, even though the distance and apparent speed of the train make that probability seem rather low; usually, they will wait to cross after the train passes, even though they may feel a little ambivalent or frustrated. This is not as true of teens, who are more likely to feel there is plenty of time to get across the track. They may recall having run across train tracks when they were younger when the train was the same distance away, and believe there is nothing different about driving across quickly. Stalling out because of trying to spurt across is not yet in their experience and the probability of failure is not translated into real images in their mind, so they ignore it.

It is therefore important that parents do not assume too much about the use of information in control of behaviors. Young people need facts in order to help them form opinions to guide their behavior, but they also need continuing support in how to use such information.

Ultimately, parents must get across to young people that the decision to have sex is the same as saying that they are willing to take on right now the responsibility of having and caring for a child for the next eighteen years; or that they are willing to take on right now having to live with an incurable sexually transmitted disease for the rest of their life; or that they are willing, right now, to give up the ability to have a child later on. Although such things may not happen to them, they are happening to an increasing number of young people. And once young people begin having sex, there is absolutely nothing to guarantee that they will not be one of those young people. Parents must stress that no method of birth control is 100 percent effective against pregnancy or sexually transmitted infections.

Adolescent Social/Emotional Changes

Lack of conceptualization of the future is also affected by some of the social/emotional changes adolescents experience as they go through puberty. Adolescents become egocentric. They feel much of the world revolves around them and how they are feeling. They become more sensitive than they will be at any other time of their lives.

One feeling they have is that they are "onstage." Everyone is watching them: everything they do, everything they say. It becomes embarrassing just to walk across a classroom. Should they wake up in the morning with a pimple on their nose, it can precipitate a whole crisis—should they even go to school that day. They feel very vulnerable. Criticism is very difficult for them to take because everything becomes so personal. The desire to fit in and be accepted increases their sense of wanting to be and act like everyone else.

Part of this egocentrism generates another feeling, that of being unique, of being different. "No one has ever felt the way I feel, no one has ever experienced what I am experiencing." That is why, when parents try to empathize by saying, "I know how you feel," young people immediately reject this as impossible. Parents who try to draw comparisons by saying, "When I was your age . . ." also fail to communicate; the adolescent sees no similarity between that example and who they are.

Because they feel so unique, so different, they don't believe what happens to other people will happen to them. For example, they think, "I know that kids who have sex can get a sexually transmitted infection. But it won't happen to me." In many ways, this feeling of being different from others leads some young people to feel immune to the things that happen to others. Indeed they almost feel immortal. When negative things do occur, they are genuinely surprised. "I didn't think it would happen to me," is the way they express it. "I didn't think I would get pregnant, at least not from doing it just one time." Others will say, "We just took a chance," not really believing that the chance would not work out for them. Parents must understand that this egocentric phase is a normal part of adolescent growth and development, but must be aware of it so that continually they can reinforce the notion that the young person is not invulnerable and that things can happen.

Moral Growth and Development

Another developmental phase that is not completed until years after puberty is that of moral growth. Moral development is a process like other phases of growth and development.

Young children are initially concerned only with self, and make decisions based on what will happen to them. Only as they grow and mature can they understand that morally they have an obligation to consider not only themselves but others. As they grow from childlike moral decisions into a consideration of others, such moral thoughts beyond themselves initially relate more to peers, people whom they know. Later on, they begin to guide their behavior based on an understanding of the need of the community for moral order. Moral growth eventually leads to understanding the broader societal implications of decision-making and behavioral control.

At first, when children are young, morally they are most concerned about what is going to happen to *them*—particularly negative things. They use this as a guide for behavior. Parents naturally know young people's limitations in this area and help them control their behavior by pointing out what "bad" thing might happen if the child followed its impulses. "If you touch that pot, it's hot and you'll get burned," parents say; or, "If you run out in the street, you'll get hit by a car."

As young people grow and mature, they can begin to think beyond negatives to guide their behavior. However, that initial way of looking at how to make moral decisions is so familiar that they often view their acts in this manner, not thinking beyond this stage. With respect to sexual behavior, they may weigh their decision with thoughts such as: "If my parents ever found out I was having sex, they'd kill me." They are not thinking of their moral responsibility for any child that may result from intercourse or how such a decision might affect their parents and others about them. The decision is based strictly on what they perceive the immediate negative consequences for *them* might be. "If I don't have sex with my boyfriend, he may stop being my boyfriend," is another example of such thinking.

Before the time of puberty, most young people are able to add the concept of reward to their moral thinking. In adolescence this gets expressed as, "Everyone respects me and I've got a good reputation, so I'm not going to risk it by having sexual intercourse right now"; or, "My religion teaches that it's wrong to have sex outside marriage and I want to look good in the eyes of the Lord." But young people still think a lot about punishment. "I can have more fun *without* the hassle and worry of sex—plus my parents would ground me forever if they found out I was having sex!"

During adolescence, however, moral decision-making begins to include others for the first time. Because peers are very important to young people, young people are more likely to emphasize consideration of peers in their moral decision-making. One aspect of this is shown by how often young people justify their decisions by saying, "But everyone's doing it." If their peers are doing it, it makes the behavior seem more morally right to them. In adulthood one doesn't do things just because one's neighbors are doing them. Adults have their own individual standards of morality which guide their behavior.

Another characteristic of the early stages of moral decision-making is the adolescent's perception of responsibility with respect to decisions. The adolescent reasons that if one didn't consciously set out to do something that might be considered wrong, then one can be excused for such behavior. "We didn't *mean* to have sex, we just got carried away." Girls may even say, "I didn't mean to get pregnant," as if somehow this excuses the behavior and makes it more morally acceptable. Adults generally have moved beyond this stage of moral thinking and guide their decisions and actions in such a manner as to recognize they are fully responsible for their behavior regardless of the circumstances. Parents need to recognize that adolescents may well be at the lower stages of moral development, where they focus on the concept of "intentions" as a moral guide.

Adult moral decision-making embodies several other unique characteristics. Adults generally guide their behavior based on an understanding of the need of their community for law and order. They understand they have an obligation to contribute to the community's well-being. They understand that they have an obligation to any child they bring into the world. They realize that although, individually, certain behavior may not make a difference, if everyone engaged in such behavior, chaos would result; therefore, they refrain. Moral growth eventually leads to an understanding of the broader societal implications of decision-making and behavioral control. For example, there are couples who have decided not to bear children of their own because of their concerns about overpopulation in the world or because of their concerns about the many "special needs" children who usually do not find adoptive homes. This latter is an example of an advanced level of moral development in that such a decision goes beyond law and order and embodies the notion of general societal good.

However, it would be meaningless to say to an adolescent, "You ought not to have sex tonight because of overpopulation in the world." Although the adult might be concerned about the world population and the risk of an unplanned, unwanted pregnancy, the adolescent may still be at the level of "Everybody's doing it" or "If my parents ever found out I'd had sex, they'd kill me" as a guide for decision-making, and therefore is unable to grasp and apply the higher level concepts to their own behavior.

Parents can help adolescents move forward in their moral development by understanding that children must procede through each stage (they don't skip them) but are always attracted to the next level. Therefore, the parent can present moral reasoning on the next level to help the child move forward. If the young person is viewing a decision based only on punishment, the parents can help them see reward as well as punishment. If the young person sees decision-making only in the light of peer behavior or the general notion of everybody's doing it, the parent can explain why it is important not to do things just because everyone's doing it. To counteract such thinking, they can also marshall facts to show that *not* everyone is doing it. The parent can explain why intentions are not sufficient rationale for behavior.

Until moral development has progressed sufficiently for the adolescent to adopt decision-making beyond concern for self and peers, he or she will not approach decision-making as does the adult, and will be more vulnerable to social and peer pressures.

In sum, while moral, cognitive, and psycho-social growth is incomplete, young people will continue to need parental supervision, guidance, and support. However, by being more aware of various characteristics of adolescent growth and development, the parent can be more sensitive to what may be motivating their young person's attitudes and behaviors. Moreover, through increased understanding of the normal limitations of their adolescents' decision-making ability, they can better assess how to help the young person who is confronted with choices. Finally, they will be more aware and appreciative of the progress their adolescent is making toward adult functioning.

2

Changes During Early Adolescence

In going from childhood to adulthood, the adolescent must accomplish certain tasks. In general, during early adolescence (twelve to fourteen years of age) young people still depend on their parents for decision-making. The central task of early adolescence is for young people to adjust to changes in their body and to become comfortable with their new body image.

Mid-adolescence (around the ages of fourteen to sixteen) tends to be the most unsettled period. Conflicts with parents increase and peer groups become more dominant in decision-making and in determining the standards of behavior. This stems from the fact that in middle adolescence the main task for young people is to establish independence.

It is in late adolescence (age seventeen and above) that young people usually attain a more secure sense of who they are and realign their relationships with their parents from a child-to-parent level to an adult-to-adult level. During late adolescence the central task young people have to accomplish is to establish self-identity.

Each adolescent goes through these adolescent changes at a rate that is normal for him or her, and not necessarily at the same rate as their peers. Parents should therefore not be upset if an adolescent appears to be out of step with his or her friends.

Early Adolescence

Most of us want to be like other people, but during adolescence this wish becomes a driving force. To the adolescent to be different means to be inferior. Yet since there is considerable variation among the young person's peers, to be alike is not always possible. However, such differences make most adolescents uneasy. Developing sexuality plays an important part in this. Deviations from the usual (what the peer group considers normal) may cause boys to wonder about their virility and girls to wonder about their femininity.

Boys most often judge how they are progressing toward manhood by outward physical signs such as: appearance of beard, hair on the body, broadening shoulders, deepening voice, development of muscles, increased height and size of sexual organs, and ability to have orgasm. Girls, too, tend to judge their progress toward womanhood by physical signs. They pay attention to breast size, change in hips, and the beginnings of menstruation. Young people whose bodily development differs from the usual often end up wondering, "What's wrong with me?" and "How do I fit into the world?"

Handling sexuality during a period in which there is a strong drive to fit in and be accepted and be alike can make teens very vulnerable. If they believe their bodily image does not fit, they sometimes try to make their behaviors more alike in order to fit in. However, stress arises not only from the necessity to cope with changes in their bodies but from the need to adjust to new biological needs and expectations as well.

Pubertal Changes

In the transition from childhood to adulthood, puberty starts near the beginning. It is the result of a complex set of biochemical changes. The pituitary gland, sometimes referred to as the "master gland," secretes the growth hormone that is responsible for changes in size, weight, body proportions, and strength. In a girl, this gland also stimulates the production of sex hormones by the ovaries, causing the girl to develop breasts, pubic hair, and begin to menstruate. In a boy, the master gland stimulates the testes to produce sex hormones that enlarge the penis and testes and cause pubic hair to grow and sperm to be produced. The physical changes of puberty extend over an eight- to ten-year period and generally end with the completion of skeletal growth in the mid- to late teens for girls and late teens to early twenties for boys.

For girls puberty begins somewhere between ages nine and sixteen; for boys it begins somewhere between ages ten and seventeen. The bodily changes that adolescents go through may bring feelings of insecurity, anxiety, shame, delight, pride, and stress. Girls experience a sequence of body changes that encompass: increase in size of breasts, appearance of straight pubic hair, growth of internal and external sex organs, growth spurt, replacement of straight pubic hair by curly pubic hair, onset of menstruation, and growth of underarm hair.

Sequential changes in boys going through puberty are: growth of internal and external sex organs, appearance of straight pubic hair, early voice changes, first ejaculation (generally ages thirteen to fifteen), replacement of straight pubic hair by curly pubic hair, rapid general growth, underarm hair, marked voice changes, and development of a beard.

Adjusting to Changes in Their Bodies

Adolescents may temporarily become preoccupied with adjusting to bodily image. Endless hours may be spent in front of the mirror examining the emerging physical self. Because the image presented by society most often differs dramatically from that presented in the mirror, the self-esteem of young people often suffers. Young people want different hair, different facial features, more or less body shape, more or less height. Falling so far from the ideal may contribute to the depression that is common to adolescents. However, by the time they reach eighteen or nineteen young people are more realistic with respect to body image and realize they are stuck with what they've got. They may say to themselves, "I may not be the prettiest girl, but I've got a great smile"; or, "I may not be as thin as most models but my hair is gorgeous." Boys, too, begin to assess themselves realistically. For example, they may feel that their muscles make up for lack of height or that their sense of humor overcomes the fact that they are thin. Until they become accepting, however, teens are vulnerable to criticism related to bodily image and can suffer lowered self-esteem because of it.

Bodily changes further stimulate the desire of teens to learn new social behaviors and roles. They may not feel adult but they definitely feel less childlike, and seek ways to express those feelings in actions.

Variances in Growth and Development

Growth and development among young people varies widely. There can be as much as a six-year difference between an early-maturing girl and a late-maturing boy. Growth and development within each individual can vary too. For example, social or emotional development can lag behind or precede physical development. Some girls or boys may actually be quite mature, yet still "stuck inside" little-girl or little-boy bodies. Their parents, teachers, and other adults may be unwilling to give them additional responsibility or respect their attitudes or feelings as much as they deserve because they view them as more childlike than adult. On the other hand, rapidly developing boys may be given too much responsibility or too much mature behavior can be expected of them just because their size makes them appear more mature.

In particular, girls who go through puberty early may experience breast development that leads them to look more mature than is their actual social or emotional development. As a consequence, they may receive inappropriate attention from boys and may have a difficult time knowing how to handle it. Some may withdraw. There are some girls who wear jackets in class or walk and sit with rounded shoulders for one or two grades so as to de-emphasize their breasts. Others may reach out for attention and engage in behaviors that are confusing for them and have little meaning except some form of perceived popularity. Girls who develop early are sometimes less highly regarded by other girls. Some studies show that girls who develop early have lower self-esteem than other girls.

On the other hand, boys who go through puberty early may have increased self-esteem as their physical size may permit them to be better athletically than their peers. Often these boys receive a great deal of attention from peers, may get elected to class offices, etc. Later on, however, as the natural athletic stars go through puberty and surpass them, such early-maturing boys may have problems as they try to adjust to a revised self-image. Late-maturing boys may actually be psychologically more flexible as adults since they have to work harder for acceptance from peers.

Special Concerns of Adolescents

A special concern adolescents may experience as they approach puberty or enter it is whether or not they are "normal." Indeed, since during early adolescence to be different means that something is wrong with one, there is a great drive toward being similar to others, for having the same experiences as others at the same time.

Puberty causes a whole set of special fears about what is in the range of normalcy. Sometimes a pressure toward sexual involvement comes from a fear that the young person may be homosexual. With homosexuality so much in the news, it is impossible for teens not to know it exists. Teens need a clear definition of homosexuality to allay their fears. They need to have it explained that homosexuality is a sexual preference for a person of the same sex. Physical curiosity about, or liking or admiring others of the same sex, does not mean that they will become homosexual. This is especially important information for younger youth in that, just before puberty, young people normally experience an attraction for a peer of their same sex. Girls can admire each other, thinking a friend is especially pretty or attractive. They can hold hands or hug each other. Boys can also find each other attractive and put their arms around each other.

Young people can be helped to become comfortable with the idea that they will have same-sex friends their whole lives. Some of their same-sex friends will be people for whom they will feel genuine love and affection. Having such feelings, however, will not mean that they will want to relate to them sexually. Young people need to know that there is nothing abnormal in deeply caring about same-sex friends. This can go a long way toward reducing sexual involvement as a backlash against homosexual fears.

Another special concern to adolescents can be their increasing interest in their own body and how it feels and responds. One particular concern may be the physical stimulation of their own body, most commonly stimulation or rubbing of the genital organs. Usually males stimulate their penis and females stimulate their clitoris. Myths are still common and young people may hear that such behavior will make them crazy, cause blindness, cause hair to grow on their palms, or cause them to become a homosexual. Young people need to know that the majority of people at one time of their life or another have done this, and that it is a normal behavior. Young people also need to know that they are also normal if they do *not* engage in such behavior.

The most common reasons for physical stimulation of one's own body are for pleasure or to relieve sexual tension or stress. Throughout adolescence, many young people may temporarily use this behavior to handle sexual feelings and reduce the likelihood of their becoming sexually involved. Young people who have sex sometimes say the "big deal" they were led to believe they would experience in having sex was greatly overrated. They wish someone had let them know that they could have satisfied their curiosity about the physical sensation of an orgasm in another way. Since sexual intercourse among young people, is done, many times, very hurriedly and with a lot of clothes on, girls, in particular, often find the experience unsatisfying or disappointing.

Another special concern for boys and girls may be penis size or size of breasts. Young people need to be assured that body shape and size are not the same as being sexual and that body shape and size do not determine ability to successfully relate sexually to another person. If young people can be helped to feel confident about their sexual growth and development, it can reduce feelings of the need to experiment or prove anything to themselves or others.

Males experience erections from infancy on. However, of special concern to boys can be the increasing number of erections they experience during the early teen years. An erection occurs when blood flows into the spongy tissue of the penis. When the blood flows out, the penis returns to its regular size.

Another new experience for boys as the result of puberty is the release of semen through the erect penis during sleep. Boys need to have it explained that erections can result from sights, thoughts, or feelings, even if these thoughts or feelings are at a barely conscious level. It is even normal for young men to get erections for no apparent reason at all. At night it is a normal process for erections to occur and even for semen to be ejaculated. These "wet dreams" generally begin around age fourteen (some boys begin as early as ten or as late as seventeen). Boys need to know that this is normal and that mothers as well as fathers know about such things.

Nevertheless, it is important that boys and girls know it is not necessary to release sperm every time an erection occurs, and that there is no harm if this is not done. It is also important that boys know they have no control over erections and that although sometimes they occur at embarrassing times, this too is normal and most people understand that this happens.

A special concern to girls is not only when they begin to menstruate but how their periods affect them. They have concerns about whether or not it is normal to have cramping and how much cramping. They have concerns about on how many days they have their periods and what happens on those days. They also have concerns about the frequency of their periods. Young girls, in particular, are irregular in their cycle and length of period. This can make it difficult for them to plan and can also cause embarrassing incidents. Parents should help girls understand that there is a wide range of "normal," but that undue discomfort should be evaluated by a doctor as no one these days need suffer because of the ovulatory cycle.

Girls also need to understand that their feelings may fluctuate because of the hormonal changes associated with their menstrual cycle. Feeling "down" just before their period or so starved that they want to eat everything in sight are two examples. Assisting girls in identifying their own feeling changes can help them understand what is happening and give them more control over actions that might flow from such feelings. Boys are sometimes perplexed by the premenstrual moods of girls, and talking to them about the subject can assuage their puzzlement and also help them to be more understanding.

Reproductive Responsibilities

Just as wet dreams in the male are the first obvious sign of sexual functioning in the boy, menstruation in girls is frequently the first obvious sign that the female reproductive organs are functioning. Girls need to understand that menstruation means that their body has begun the process of each month preparing an egg cell to be fertilized so that a baby can be born. They need to understand that there is no harm to the body when the egg cell is not fertilized and that the egg cell (which is no bigger than the head of a pin) is absorbed back into the body and then flushed out with the lining of the uterus that was built up in preparation for the egg cell, had it been fertilized. The fluid and tissue that comes out of the girls' body at the time of menstruation is the unneeded lining of the uterus.

Biological Maturity Means New Responsibilities

Both boys and girls need to understand that once the reproductive system has started functioning, they carry a new responsibility. Boys and girls need to know that a pregnancy can result if a boy ejaculates sperm cells in or near the girl's vagina. Such sperm cells are able to travel to the fallopian tube inside the girl's body and unite with an egg cell if one is there. Pregnancy is most likely to occur if sexual intercourse occurs two weeks before the beginning of the girl's next period, which is generally when an egg cell is released. However, an egg cell may be released at unusual times during the menstrual cycle and therefore whenever one has intercourse there is a chance of becoming involved in a pregnancy. Further, sperm cells can live within the girl's body for as long as seven days. Indeed, humans are designed to be a very fertile species; over the course of one year, 90 percent of females having intercourse will become pregnant. Some will become pregnant the very first time they have sexual intercourse.

Parents therefore need to stress the responsibility that goes along with a maturing body. They need to stress that although the reproductive organs generally mature early in the change from childhood to adulthood, this does not mean that the individual is prepared physically, emotionally, socially, or financially to become a parent. Successfully handling the feelings and curiosity that accompany the beginning of their reproductive capacity is one way for adolescents to show they are becoming mature.

Adolescents are very sensitive to their body processes. Providing information and reassurance that they are, in fact, normal and that taking responsibility for their reproductive capacity is a normal function can be reassuring to young people. Parents might even say, "You know, the changes you are going through are changes your great-grandparents went through, your grandparents went through, your dad (mom) and I went through. So gaining the capacity to reproduce isn't unique to you. We have all had to adjust to these changes. Each generation does. Your children will too.

"Learning to take responsibility for that reproductive capacity is something we all had to do too—just as you are learning to do. However, since times change, what will be unique to you will be the environment in which you must think and act responsibly and the ways available to you to help you carry out responsible behavior. I can share some experiences I've had with you and give you some tips, if you want them. Regardless, I'm confident you can learn to manage that responsibility well, just as the vast majority of people do."

The Importance of Accurate Information

It is important that young people be provided with clear, accurate information about the reproductive aspect of their bodies. Young people may be more involved with the obvious external sexual development than the internal one. They need to know exactly what changes the internal reproductive organs have undergone so that they can begin to integrate knowledge and control of that capacity into their thoughts and actions.

Parents should be clear and use correct terms when they give young people such information. One young girl's mother had told her very carefully that a man had seeds and that when he planted them in a woman's body, a baby grew. Later on, this bewildered pregnant girl protested, "But he didn't have any seeds." Parents who give general warnings, such as "Don't fool around" or "Don't get a girl in trouble," leave young people in great confusion. Young people often then don't know what they can and what they can't do. Some suffer needlessly, thinking that even such mild behavior as kissing can lead to pregnancy, while others take risks because they rely on myths such as "You can't get someone pregnant if you do it standing up."

Young people need to have intercourse clearly defined for them: They need to know this is when a male puts his penis into a female's vagina. They need to know that a liquid called semen comes out of the tip of the penis and that the liquid contains sperm cells that can cause a pregnancy. They need to know specifically that if sperm cells are released in or near the vagina, a pregnancy can occur. They need to know that even without ejaculation, small amounts of sperm may leak out as the penis gets ready to ejaculate and that these may cause a pregnancy.

Information About Sexually Transmitted Diseases Is Important Too

They also need to know that infections can be spread through sexual intercourse. They need to know that if either young person has ever had sex before with someone who had a sexually transmitted infection, or otherwise has come in contact with bodily fluids of someone who had certain kinds of sexually transmitted infections, that person may pass on the infection. Therefore, it needs to be stressed over and over again that sexual behavior has consequences. It is also important for young people to know that some kinds of sexually transmitted infections have no symptoms and that, left untreated, they can damage the young person's capacity to have children later in life. They also need to know that although the majority of sexually transmitted infections, when diagnosed early, can be treated, there are two that currently are incurable. One is herpes. The other is AIDS.

It is important that young people know that there are ways to reduce the likelihood of an infection being passed or a pregnancy occurring and that these methods fall under the category referred to as birth control or contraceptives. But it is equally important to say that no method is 100 percent sure and that anyone who has sexual intercourse takes some risk.

The condom, or "rubber," is the main recommended

method of reducing the risk of the spread of sexually transmitted infections. The condom can help reduce the risk of pregnancy as well. This is a method used by the male. Nevertheless, it must be made clear to young people that condoms only reduce the risk, they do not eliminate it. Even when they use condoms, young people can still get or spread a sexually transmitted infection or become involved in a pregnancy.

Other kinds of contraceptives (pills, foams, creams, sponges, diaphragms, jellies) all must be used by the female. Although some, such as contraceptive foam, may contribute in a limited way to preventing the spread of some kinds of sexually transmitted infections, the primary purpose of the contraceptive methods used by the female is to keep the egg and sperm from uniting, so that a pregnancy cannot occur. It is important to stress that these methods of birth control also only *reduce* the risk of pregnancy, they do not *eliminate* it.

Young people therefore need to know that because sexual intercourse cannot be made fully safe from pregnancy or spread of infection yet, it is best entered into only by people who can carry full responsibility for living with and handling any consequences of that behavior. Having to live with or handle such consequences at a young age can interfere with, delay, or even thwart young people's natural progress toward becoming mature and independent.

Young people need to know that they cannot tell if a person has a sexually transmitted infection by just looking at him/her. They need to know that if they have sexual intercourse with someone who has had sexual intercourse with others, they are exposing themselves to the germs of everyone else with whom that person has had intercourse— even if that person had intercourse only once over five years ago.

What Can Parents Do

Parents can give young people accurate and adequate factual information so that they will not be encouraged to experiment and find out on their own.

Parents can make sure their adolescent knows that hope is insufficient. Hoping a person does not have a sexually transmitted infection or hoping they don't get involved in a pregnancy is not enough. It is the same as saying they are willing to let those things happen.

Parents need to help young people understand that beliefs will not be enough either. Believing the wonderful person they are dating could not possibly have a sexually transmitted infection, believing "It won't happen to me," is not enough. They must believe it can happen to them.

Parents need to help young people understand that not deciding about sexual behavior and "letting things happen" *is*, in effect, deciding. Intending not to do something and then doing it is the same as deciding to do it.

Finally, parents must stress that once a person is biologically mature, he or she must assume responsibility for that capability. He or she must use that capacity in a way that will not harm themselves or harm others in any way.

3

Mid-Adolescence, Late Adolescence and Sexuality

Mid-adolescence (fourteen to sixteen years of age), in which there is a strong drive for independence, causes some special problems for both young people and parents with respect to the management of sexuality. Some of the upheaval adolescents and their families experience comes from the social pressure adolescents feel during this time, as well as from their emerging identification with the independence of adults. Adolescents may find themselves confused or uncertain about achieving independence. They may desire the freedom of independence but also want the sense of security associated with dependence. Vacillation and confusing feelings can make the period stormy for both adolescents and parents. Behaviors can come in stops and starts. Since growth does not generally occur in a smooth, synchronized manner, both parents and their children are often left not knowing what to expect.

During middle adolescence, although there is a continued need for dependence and emotional support, there is a gradual loosening of ties. Not until late adolescence is the process more or less complete. Most people have difficulty in reading correctly the signals that young people send about their growing need for detachment. In part this is because at the same time they are striving toward more independent functioning, they have continued needs for adults who will permit emotional dependence and who will set limits.

Sexuality in middle and late adolescence can become mixed up with the issues of independence and the need for detachment from the family. Unfortunately, sexual behavior can become the battleground on which such issues are worked through. Teens may come to see it as the one area in which they can rebel or assert freedom and independence.

The Importance of Peers

It is important that parents understand the meaning of the peer group to teens. Peers play an essential role in the change from childhood to adulthood. Trying to establish their own identity—one that is separate from their family—is too difficult for most adolescents without the benefit of peer interaction and support. At around age twelve adolescents begin to move away from the parents who have supported and protected them all their lives. It is in peer groups that adolescents work for recognition, check out new standards and principles, make new judgments about what is right and what is wrong. They shift the need for support and commendation from family (from adults) to peers. Involvement with peers thus is one of the most important ways that adolescents find to help them separate from their parents in order to become independent-functioning adults.

Venturing out from childhood before they have a firm growing sense of an adult self would be all but impossible for most youth unless they could use the lifeline of peers. In particular, since human beings are social animals—especially when young—adolescents must have some connection in a social setting, some other person or persons to sustain them, for them to be with. It is important at this time for them to try their new selves out in ways that are cognitive, emotional, and social. This is a time when adolescents look to peers, perhaps to a particular friend, with whom they can share their changing self.

Around age twelve, when they first seek out peers, boys still pair up with boys, and girls with girls. At age twelve and thirteen, young people are much more comfortable with a friend of their own sex than they are with someone of the opposite sex. Although they may be eager for heterosexual relationships, they generally are not ready for them. Relatively soon, however, young people's inclination may be to try to seek out someone of the opposite sex.

During mid-adolescence, some young people develop almost inseparable relationships with someone of the opposite sex. These relationships may not be based on sexual attraction so much as a companionship through which to achieve independence from family. By finding acceptance from another person outside their family, teens can more readily accept themselves and find the confidence to distance themselves from family. Hence, peers are absolutely essential to the healthy changeover from childhood to adulthood.

It is in the peer grouping that the adolescent gets to test out and try out a new self. At this time, adolescents may withhold information from their parents and refuse to share even some basic things. At the same time, with friends, adolescents can endlessly discuss ideas, feelings, behaviors, other youth—all of which serves to help them sort out who they are, what they think, and what they feel. They listen to other young people to see what ideas, attitudes, values, and behaviors appeal to them. This is a time for experimenting, for trying on various new aspects of identity to see what fits and what doesn't. It is a time of pushing outward at the walls of self to find out what the parameters or dimensions of the newly emerging self are.

It is a time to test out physical capacities, emotional capacities, social capacities, intellectual capacities.

Testing out this new self with peers is a more equal setting for adolescents. Parents may be physically stronger or have a greater emotional hold on the young person due to the parental role. With peers, however, there is more equality and thus a more appealing environment for examination of self. As a consequence, most experimentation with alcohol, drugs, etc., is done among peers.

Parents may be interested in knowing that this distancing from parents by adolescents to establish separate identity, first accomplished through alignment with peers, is ultimately repeated again. The second time it is necessary for the young person to distance himself or herself from peers in order to complete the process of becoming an independent adult.

Because peers play such an important role in helping the young person become independent, and can have an influence on the direction the exploration of self takes, parents often fear the peer group. Much peer influence is positive, however. Many times peers provide a good grounding in reality with respect to interpersonal relationships. Unlike family, who are expected always to be interested and caring, the teen has to *win* the respect and affection of peers.

Group Acceptance
Part of growing involves learning what prices are worth paying for group acceptance and what prices are not. Initially, most teens are unwilling to risk loss of peer approval. Hence, if a young person's curfew is 10 p.m. while his peers do not have to be home until 10:30, the young person will almost always risk parental disapproval because peer acceptance is so overwhelmingly important. Parents who see violating the curfew as an act of defiance and rebellion

against them and their rules are probably misinterpreting the behavior. Instead, it is an act of compliance with peer norms in a situation that the teen sees as necessary to his keeping his lifeline to future adulthood and independence.

Later on, as teens become more secure in who they are as persons, they will be able to abide by certain "house rules" without feeling as threatened. This following of house rules, however, will be done under a realignment of relationships within the family in which the teen will relate more to his parents as an adult than as a child. The house rules therefore are followed out of respect for his parents as individuals and their rights in their own home, rather than as arbiters of acceptable behavior.

Peers, Sexuality, and Sexual Behavior

Within the peer setting, as part of finding out who they are, teens may want to test out their capacity for physical intimacy as well as emotional intimacy. Indeed, one important task of adolescence is to establish a meaningful relationship with someone outside the family. Establishing their capacity to relate to someone in this manner assures them they will be able to find a mate as an adult. Sometimes this person actually becomes their adult mate. More often, such a relationship serves as the reference point on which future relationships are built.

Part of distancing oneself from the family and establishing identity as a man or a woman is done through learning how to relate to people of the opposite sex, not just as a person but as a male or as a female. In times past, there was a prolonged period of learning to do this in groups rather than through individual dating; today young people move more quickly into individual dating and they begin dating at a younger age.

Furthermore, although dating the same person over a lengthy period of time usually provided opportunities for close physical contact, such behavior was generally limited. Today, more teens accept sexual intercourse as part of dating behavior. Some feel, "It's just a part of growing up." Others feel, "Everybody's doing it." Further, many feel that a long dating relationship is not necessary before intercourse. Peers play an important role in such attitudes.

Studies indicate that those young people who do not have intercourse believe that fewer of their peers are engaging in such behavior than do those who have intercourse. They also are less likely to think that their best friend is having sex. Those who are not having sex also indicate that they feel that their friends are less likely to approve of that behavior. Obviously, therefore, peer influence can also be helpful in helping a teen postpone sexual involvement.

Parental Influence on Peers

Parents cannot choose their children's friends for them. Over time, however, parents may influence what kinds of friends the young person associates with. Parents who feel their adolescent is spending too much time with a group of young people who are more likely to engage in sexual behavior may want to structure opportunities for their child to relate to peers whose values and beliefs and actions seem closer to those that they wish their children to have. It is much easier to do this early—before the relationship with a negative peer group is deeply formed or the desire to be independent has become overwhelming.

Having more than one peer group—neighborhood group, school group, church youth group, youth organization group—can be helpful to a young person in weighing pressures and actions. Parents who try to limit their child's association with certain peers will be much more successful if the young person is integrated into more than one peer group. If parents are not sensitive to the needs of their child for peer support and unwisely disrupt the only peer relationships a young person has, it can serve as a focal point for adolescent rebellion. Some parents take such drastic actions as sending their child to another school, or to live temporarily with relatives, if they feel the young person has chosen an overwhelmingly negative peer group or has few choices but peers the parents disapprove of. However, adolescents who can be helped to make good judgments about people and resist pressures to conform will be stronger adults and will learn lessons that sometime in life must be learned.

Other ways parents cope are by using parental controls to limit their children's engagement in certain kinds of activities with peers. The young person may resent being the only one who has to come home after the football game, but it does not necessarily mean that he or she will be dropped by the peer group.

Joint problem-solving or decision-making with other parents of a particular peer group is another way parents can help avoid certain problems. For example, if all parents agree that their youth cannot go to parties unless there is a known adult present to supervise, the burden of sanction does not fall on any one particular youth or his or her parents. Still, again it must be stressed that peers can be equally positive influences. Peers can help teens set limits. If peers view certain negative behaviors as unacceptable, it is they who exert the pressure that can prevent or change the behavior. When such pressures come from the peer group, they may be more readily accepted by the young person.

Some peer influence may be structured. One way is for the parent to integrate the young person into a peer group that is likely to exert pressure against behaviors such as sexual intercourse. Another way is for parents to lobby for programs or activities in their school and community for their child and other young people that use the "social and peer influence" model.

Formal Programs Using Positive Peer Influence

These new educational programs that use positive peer influence are the result of two realities. One is the experience with deficits in previous prevention models. The other is improved understanding of the importance of social and peer pressures with respect to adolescent behaviors.

Adults originally assumed that giving young people factual information would be sufficient as a way of influencing adolescent behavior. For example, early drug programs gave information about drugs and their harmful effects, on the assumption that it was merely out of ignorance that young people began using drugs. Early sex education programs used the same fact-giving approach, believing that it was because young people lacked information on how pregnancy occurred or about the negative consequences of adolescent pregnancy that they risked such an occurrence. Research in both fields showed that young people learned a great deal in such programs, but they did not change their behavior.

The next generation of programs gave factual content but placed a new emphasis on decision-making skills, believing that if young people were taught a formal strategy for looking at choices, weighing alternatives, and evaluating outcomes, they would better be able to make decisions about behavior. These programs, too, did not seem to impact sufficiently on behavior the way program planners had hoped.

Yet another generation of programs was based on the premise that if young people's personal understanding could be increased, they would be able to make better decisions and use factual information differently. Such programs focused variously on enabling young people to examine and clarify values, helping them set goals, facilitating their identification of positive aspects of their personality and abilities that would make them feel good about themselves, or improving their ability to communicate with others. These programs, too, failed to show clear-cut results regarding behavior.

The latest generation of programs is based on the notion that in large measure youth begin negative health behaviors because of social and peer influences. Such influences come from the general society along with peer attitudes and behaviors.

One example of a program that uses the peer influence model is the Postponing Sexual Involvement Educational Program developed by the author and others in Atlanta, Georgia. The Postponing Program uses older teens (eleventh- and twelfth-grade students) to present information on postponing sexual involvement to younger teens (those under sixteen). Through dialogue, peer group interaction, and modeling by the older teens, young teens are helped to deal with social and peer pressures to become sexually involved.

As part of the Postponing Sexual Involvement Educational Program, the older teen leaders help younger teens identify where social pressures to have sex come from. For example, they help young people examine the messages they get about sexual involvement from what they see on television and in the movies, what they hear in their music, and the behaviors of admired adults such as movie stars or rock musicians. They help teens distinguish between the fantasy world created by the media and the real world in which teens must live. The older teens also help the younger teens understand why so much advertising contains sexual messages and how to cut through those messages so that they won't be influenced to do something they do not wish to do.

The older teens also spend time helping younger teens deal with peer pressures to become sexually involved. They increase the understanding of younger teens about motivations behind peer pressure. They help younger teens think about ways to handle pressure situations. Finally, the older teen leaders teach younger teens assertive steps for saying no and help them practice those skills.

When youth are grouped and given messages about postponing sexual involvement by older teens, along with being given opportunities to engage in mutual problem-solving and to practice ways of carrying out positive behavior, peer pressure toward beginning negative behaviors can be reduced. Indeed, most often peer pressure toward responsible behavior can be positively increased. The modeling provided by the older teens can reassure younger teens that not everyone is "doing it" and that one can "*not* do it" and survive. One can even be an admired and respected person.

Boys can learn that there are older successful boys who feel strongly that having sex at a young age is inappropriate and can "mess up" one's chances for the future. Girls can learn that giving in and having sex when they really don't want to is allowing themselves to be used. They can learn that there are girls who don't have sex and are popular and happy with themselves. The techniques the older teens teach the younger teens to use in saying no reinforce the belief of the younger teens that they have the skills to successfully postpone sexual involvement.

The Postponing Sexual Involvement Educational Program takes five classroom periods when presented in a school setting. Generally the older teens are selected based on principal, school counselor, and school teacher recommendations. Part of the screening process involves evaluating their written essays on why they want to become a teen leader and teach younger teens how to say no to sexual involvement. Initial presentation skills are important, but such skills are further developed when those selected to be teen leaders go through the required twenty hours of training.

Equal numbers of males and females are hired, so that the educational program can be led each time jointly by a male teen leader and female teen leader. Monthly in-services are used to help teens resolve any problems they have encountered in presenting the program. To help with any problems that might arise for which the teens are not trained, an adult thoroughly familiar with the program is always present in the classroom when the teens present the program.

Follow-up studies indicate significant differences in rates of sexual involvement among those who have had the teen-led program in contrast to matched groups of youth who have not had the teen-led program. A Postponing Sexual Involvement Program for Parents also is provided to parents so that they can reinforce the information and skills given their young teens.

Another kind of peer influence program uses teens as "peer counselors." Roughly the same age as those they are to counsel, these students are trained to provide information and help their peers with problem-solving around difficult issues. Generally these teens are not engaged in formal presentations but act informally in teen networks. Sometimes they lead group discussions in health care or school settings.

These kinds of peer teaching and counseling programs have impact by providing youth with accurate information, and skills to use the information, in ways that are acceptable to them. At the minimum, they can create an understanding for a wider range of behaviors among youth and reduce the pressure toward conformity. Often such programs only are given if parents decide they want such programs and put pressure on their own peers in P.T.A. groups or schools and community agencies to make such programs available.

Helping Youth with Peers

Another way parents can help youth is by assisting them in thinking about how much influence over their life peers should have. In this connection, parents can help young teens understand the importance of developing their own beliefs and sticking to them. Ultimately, teens must realize that they are responsible for their own behavior.

Parents also can help their sons and daughters by limiting the opportunities for them to be vulnerable to peer pressures. The parent can negotiate with the young person about time spent alone with her boyfriend or his girlfriend. The rule might be that the boyfriend or girlfriend cannot come over unless a parent is at home; however, whenever a parent is at home the friend will always be welcome.

Another way parents can help their children is by helping them understand more about peer pressure. One common pressure tactic teens use is to make the young person believe that having sex as a young teen is a behavior all his or her peers are engaging in: "C'mon, everybody's doing it." Parents need to help their children not be taken in by that. Actually, there are more young people who aren't having sex than who are having sex. And, the younger the person, the more likely it is that the majority of teens in their age group are not having sex. Data presented in the media about sexual involvement among teens is often misleading because it is based on the number of young people who have ever had sex and therefore includes young people who may have had sex only once, several years before.

As important as helping their adolescent understand that not everyone his or her age is having sex is for parents to help their young person understand that many of those who are having sex really don't want to, but have let themselves get pressured into it. Indeed, some young people who try sex as young teens regret having done it and do not have sex again until they are much older.

Pressures on Boys

Parents need to appreciate the fact that often boys feel pressure from other boys to become sexually involved. They are often led to believe by their peers that there is something wrong with them, or that they may even be homosexual if they are not having sex. They also are lead to believe that they are being a man—macho or "cool"—if they have sex.

In fact, sometimes it is not just peers but fathers who encourage their sons to become a man through sexual involvement. Unfortunately, societal attitudes reinforce the notion that there is something wrong with a young man who grows to sexual maturity in today's society without becoming sexually involved. Teen-aged boys usually have received such messages from the time they were very young.

Boys in particular need to be helped to understand that there are many reasons why young people may choose not to become sexually involved. Among such reasons are:

- fear of pregnancy
- fear of sexually transmittted infection
- religious beliefs
- respect for their girlfriend or boyfriend
- not wanting to hurt their parents
- not feeling a need to have sexual intercourse

- not wanting to risk interference with future plans
- there is no one they care deeply about and are ready to make a commitment to
- they are not old enough

Boys need to know that being a real man has little to do with having sex. Being a man means being able to make a commitment to a relationship and take responsibility for the consequences of one's actions in that relationship.

Many young men find it easier to pretend they are doing things they really aren't doing, or pretend they believe things they really don't believe, than to face their peers with the truth. However, these young men might be surprised to find out how many of their peers are pretending just as they are, for social acceptance. Boys need to be helped to understand that having the courage of their own beliefs and the ability to stick up for them may actually help another person who is too timid to admit he feels the same way. If parents talk with young men about having such beliefs and standing up for them, it can make a difference. Even though they still may not publicly acknowledge that is how they feel, it can reinforce their ability to not do anything that would go against their beliefs.

Boys can also experience direct pressures from girls to become sexually involved. And because of the various attitudes about men and sex, it can be more difficult for a boy to say no to sexual involvement than a girl. Also it is hard for boys to say no because they are curious and want to know what it would feel like or be like. And they may worry that they may not get another chance, or that they may turn off the girl or hurt her feelings.

It may be helpful for boys to hear that although people are alike in many ways, and that everybody is a sexual human being, people are different too. Although everybody wants to love and to be loved, needs and values may vary.

Each may want something different from life. What other people do or how they are doing it is not really what matters. What a girl may want from a relationship may not at all fit with what a boy may want. Borrowing decisions from other people is never a good idea. It is important in becoming a man for the young person to make up his own mind. He is the person who has to live with the consequences of the way he acts.

Sometimes boys can use physical sex as a way of avoiding having a close, caring relationship. However, preparation for adult life, including marriage and parenthood, requires developing the capacity to care in a relationship and be responsible. Avoiding emotional and psychological closeness closes off some important learning experiences with respect to what relationships are all about.

Sometimes boys become so involved with sexual thoughts and feelings that they focus on sex almost exclusively. They need to be helped to think of sex as a part of life—but only a part. It is not separate from everything else. In sex, as in other aspects of life, part of becoming an adult is learning to respect themselves and to respect other people. They need to learn that, as in other relationships, those between a male and female involve consideration and trust. They also need to learn that there is much more to male–female relationships than sexuality.

Pressures on Girls

Girls are under peer pressures too. For example, girls can get pressure from other girls: "What? You haven't done it yet, girl? What's the matter with you?" Some girls get tricked into believing "the first time" is not important, so they give in just to "get it over with." Sometimes girls have sex to try to cure loneliness or unhappiness; They may think having sex will make them more popular.

Sex does not really resolve any of these problems. In

some cases it can even make matters worse. Finding solutions to loneliness or unhappiness, or the lack of popularity, does not come through sexual involvement but through getting to know oneself and then reaching out to include life experiences that will really help a young person become the kind of person he or she would like to be.

Parents can sometimes be helpful in bringing a new range of experiences into the lives of young people. Perhaps a shy girl might like to take karate. Perhaps a lonely girl would like to volunteer at a home for the aged. Helping young people expand their interests and abilities, and gain acceptance in whatever circumstances they can, may help alter their perspectives.

But most often the pressure on a girl to become sexually involved comes from her boyfriend. He may be curious. He may feel that he needs to have sex to satisfy his urges. He may feel he needs to show his dominance in their relationship by having sex. He may feel that having sex is the only way he can really show the girl how much he cares for her. He may be feeling pressure from his peers to prove he can make it with a girl, that he is a "man." The girl then becomes the means to enable him to brag.

Parents need to help girls think through what they really want in a relationship with a boy at this time in their lives. They need to help them think about the qualities that go into a good relationship. They need to help them think about mutual respect, understanding, and communication. Parents can help girls clarify what their attitude is about a boy who doesn't respect his girlfriend's wishes not to have sex. They also need to help her examine her feelings about girls who give in to having sex when they really don't want to.

Parents can make such discussion general, rather than personal. During a conversation about dating and pressures, they can ask, "What do you think about a boy who pressures a girl to have sex with him after she has told him she doesn't want to do that?" Many times, young people will respond with the idea that he really doesn't care about her or is just using her. Parents can follow up with, "What do you think about a girl who gives in to having sex when she really doesn't want to." Young people may respond with statements that indicate that the girl must not have a very good opinion of herself and/or is just letting herself be used.

It is important for parents to help teens think and talk about what they think it means to use someone, particularly in a sexual relationship. As part of their discussion, parents need to continually reinforce the fact that not everyone is "doing it." They need to remind teens that sometimes young people say things to try to look important in the eyes of their peers. They need to help them understand how much boys (and girls) often use "lines" to get other people to do things. Learning to recognize such statements and thinking about how to respond to them can help young people feel more confident about their attitudes and abilities. Teens need to learn that in good relationships the rights of the other person are respected. They also need to learn that it is all right to say no. There is nothing wrong with saying no, and they are not abnormal if they do so.

4

Teen Self-Concepts and Sexual Behavior

Self-confidence is one of the strongest skills that an adolescent can have to deal with peer pressure. If young people are unsure of themselves and need acceptance by peers to validate who they are, they are more likely to give in to negative peer pressure than those who have developed a good self-concept. Self-confident teens are much less likely to be flattered or frightened into doing something they are not ready for.

The Importance of Good Self-Esteem

As they grow and mature, adolescents tend to spend longer periods of time away from the family. Such time may be spent at school-related activities, part-time jobs, visiting friends, or even talking to them on the phone late into the evening. This separation from the family and broadening of activities and experiences brings about even more possibilities of successes and failures. Young people increasingly look to others outside the family for feedback about how they are faring. Their self-image and self-esteem are much more related to the responses from these non-family individuals than is the self-concept of young children who, most often, are able to get a sense of well-being from their family.

Success in school becomes very important to adolescents. This encompasses not just academic success but success in social and athletic school-related activities. Self-esteem plays a critical role in this phase of adolescent development. Most young people have formed their self-esteem from the remarks made about them or the treatment they have received in the past, as they were growing. Such treatment and remarks have come from parents, brothers, sisters, teachers, friends, relatives, neighbors. If what the child has heard and experienced has been mostly positive, he or she will have much higher self-esteem than the child who has had more or mostly negative experiences and comments.

Self-esteem is really a key measure of the person's feeling of self-worth. Self-esteem is more or less a picture of him- or herself that the adolescent carries around in his/her head. Adolescents may think of themselves as strong, attractive, happy, talented, likable and liked, smart, good, proud, capable. If young persons have a preponderance of such feelings, they will have high self-esteem. It will affect how they approach school, home, friendships, new experiences. On the other hand, the young person who feels afraid, angry, lonely, unattractive, stupid or boring will have very low self-esteem. It also affects how he or she approaches life.

Because self-esteem is an accumulation over the years of many experiences, the raising or lowering of self-esteem is often a slow process. People who feel good about themselves and have a great deal of respect for themselves are less likely to be pressured into doing things they don't want to do than are young people who do not feel very good about themselves. Helping young people deal with negative remarks or negative experiences can be an important task of parents. It is never too late to support a child's good self-esteem or try to raise a child's poor self-esteem.

Helping Young People Think and Act Positively

One trap that young people fall into is agreeing with the negative remarks they may hear about themselves. Although it may seem obvious, young people do not always know they don't have to agree with any negative statement. Parents need to teach their children to disagree and to store the positive replacement for the remark in their head.

For example, if someone says, "That's a dumb remark! Everybody knows no one waits to have sex until they're married anymore. What a turkey you are!" the young person could fall into the trap and feel, "I never make any acceptable statements. I guess they are right. I really am a nerd." The parent needs to help the teen to be able to say to himself or herself, "Wait a minute! That's not really right. I'm really good at . . ." The quick replacement of the labeling as a turkey with a positive image of self is the most important task! Proving the point is not an important task, because the issue is that the young person feels O.K. about him- or herself. If this is so, he or she will be able to believe that they have a right to make any statement they want and that they are still an O.K. person whether the statement is right or wrong. They also will be able to hold on to their belief without needing to prove it.

Another problem of young people with low self-esteem is coping with disappointments. Young people with low self-esteem are more likely to make "mountains out of molehills" when something does not go right for them. Often, the young person has the feeling that everything always goes right for everyone else and always goes wrong for him/her. The adolescent doesn't recognize that everyone has disappointments and that people have disappointments all the time. However, the person with high self-esteem is able to say, "I wish I'd been invited to the dance after the football game. Oh well, I'm not the only one who's not going. Maybe I'll be invited to the next one, particularly if I keep walking from English to Math with that new boy." The young person with low self-esteem says, "What do I care? Those dances are stupid. I wouldn't go, even if someone asked me."

Parents can help young people realize that thinking about themselves in positive ways is more helpful to their self-esteem than not. Parents can suggest that young people start the day by purposely reminding themselves about their good points and the things they know they are capable of. The teen can tell him- or herself, "I am pretty good— period. I really like myself. I like being a responsible person. I can learn from other people."

Parents can suggest that teens repeat these messages to themselves during the day. Teens need to know that if they evaluate themselves positively, others are more likely to evaluate them in that manner. Positive statements to themselves are one way of beginning to make the change to a better self-esteem. When confronted with situations that they think they can't handle, they should repeat the positive statements. They can talk to themselves about the problem too, and say, "Look I'm a capable person. I know I've got what it takes to deal with this." Parents can also help teens understand that part of being capable is getting help, if it is needed. Such understanding further increases self-esteem.

Since people with good self-esteem see themselves as people who can set goals and reach them, young people should take credit for the many things they do well. Getting homework done, giving it all they have when they try out for a team, being nice to their younger brother, making a friend all signal something accomplished. Successful people set realistic goals and feel good because they achieve them. Helping a young person recognize and take pride in small but nevertheless important accomplishments will help him or her feel successful.

What Else Parents Can Do

Forget the myth that adolescents relate only to peers. Parents remain an important base of adolescent support. Adolescents like, respect, and want to be with adults. While peers are increasingly important, adolescents still depend on adults for guidance, emotional support, a sense of identity and self-esteem, and help in solving big problems. Talk to your adolescent about making decisions about sexuality, about peer pressures, and about media messages. Do not wait until the child is a teenager to begin talking with your child.

Adults can help teens during this period in other ways too. Besides helping improve self-esteem, they can encourage responsibility. The way most of us learn to take responsibility is to be given responsibility. Parents can create opportunities for teenagers to make decisions on their own. Not all decisions that teenagers make will work out well, but they will learn as much from their mistakes as their successes. As a parent, make supportive statements rather than critical ones.

Young people may start off taking responsibility in smaller ways and gradually increase the amount and kinds they are involved in. For example, they may start off making their own lunches. Later on, they can plan the family meals for the week. They can take responsibility for choosing their own school clothes, based on a defined budget. Later, they can manage the family budget for a vacation.

Giving teens responsibility will show them that you respect them and love them and will support their growth toward independence. Nevertheless, make sure the responsibilities given teens, and the decisions they are asked to make, are within their capacities. Nothing will destroy confidence faster than consistent failure to achieve. Having a sense of responsibility and knowing they can carry it, knowing that they have good judgment and having the self-confidence to exercise it, will go a long way toward helping teens deal with peer pressure.

Parents should be aware however, that there will be times when the adolescent will want to withdraw from carrying more adult responsibilities. When the outside world gets tough, adolescents may temporarily retreat. Vacillating in their feelings of wanting autonomy and independence and at times wanting to be dependent and cared for is commonplace. Because parents become confused by what appears to be an abrogation of responsibility or a step backward from more adult functioning, they may become angry or withdraw. Adolescents, too, may become angry and non-communicative. Their self-concept may suffer because they feel inadequate in the face of becoming more adult. They may rebel against taking responsibility or handling independence in an adult way. No one, not even the seemingly more popular and well-adjusted young teens, makes it through adolescence with self-esteem intact at all times and an ever-increasing coping ability.

Understanding, Support, and Patience: Three Parental Tools

Ways to give support to children at this time may not seem clear. And yet, it is a time when youth may need the most support. Above all, be patient. Distancing from parents and being confident enough to function independently takes time, and no one accomplishes this task smoothly. Rebelling is not only inevitable, it is also healthy. Testing their limits, taking risks, questioning rules are all part of the way teenagers prove to themselves and their peers that they do have some control over their lives. Non-judgmental empathy is very important during this time: Just saying,

"I care," can make a difference. Statements such as "I may not always like what you do, but I always like you" can be supportive too, signaling to the adolescent that not all behavior is acceptable but that the adult is there for the young person in a continuing way.

Parents should remember that adolescents have a great many tasks to accomplish by eighteen or nineteen years of age, and this places a heavy burden on the adolescent. For example, by that age most adolescents will have become comfortable with their bodily changes. They will have developed a sexual identity, established sexual values, and learned what responsible sexual behavior is and how to make it part of their lives.

By eighteen or nineteen, most adolescents will have established realistic educational goals within the resources of the family: on-the-job training, trade school, or college. They will have been able to pick some things they can realistically do to earn a living based on their physical, social, and mental abilities.

By that time, most adolescents will have chosen a system of values, established a personal code of ethics, and developed a sense of right and wrong. They will have developed meaningful relationships with persons outside the family. They will have developed adult thought processes, in which they can think abstractly, conceptualize the future, and analyze their own thoughts. They will have established independence from adult authority or dominance. Such teens will have developed the ability to take responsibility, make decisions, persist when moderately frustrated, see themselves realistically, and visualize the consequences of their behavior and actions.

Finally, by eighteen or nineteen years of age teens will have established an identity. They will have developed an adult self-image—either good or bad. They will have become a leader or a follower; an introvert or extrovert. And although some sort of continuing emotional and financial dependence on their parents may remain for a period, by and large most teens will have moved into at least provisional adulthood and will take their place in the world on a more equal footing with their parents and other adults.

What to Do If the Going Gets Rough

All this is a lot to accomplish and parents should not underestimate the complexity of the changes needed to accomplish it. Parents who have special difficulties in going through the adolescent period with their children and who fear the possible sexual involvement of their child can take several steps.

One step is to know the parents of your child's friends and classmates. Form a support group of parents and other concerned adults. Not only can general concerns be addressed but specific ones; for example, parents can help each other deal with the relaxed sexual behavior among teens or the opportunities for such behavior. If parents and other adults can agree on common messages, it will reduce the comparison between standards and rules set by one home or organization and those set by another.

Another step parents can take is to work in the community to make sure there are well-supervised activities available that are appealing to a wide variety of young people. Making sure that there are fun things for young people to do in positive groups, or that there are public places where adolescent couples can go to enjoy themselves does not solve problems completely, but it can help young people avoid spending large amounts of time in private situations with little to do.

An additional step parents can take if living with their adolescent and providing appropriate guidance gets too tough is: Seek professional support. Mental-health professionals—social workers, psychologists, and psychiatrists trained in adolescent and family matters, or physicians trained in adolescent medicine—can often provide very helpful insights and advice into how to keep the family functioning. Having a child going through adolescence throws most families into some disequilibrium. Although families can adjust and restabilize themselves, mental-health support can sometimes make the process less stressful or can aid the family to get itself back together in less time than this might normally take.

Families who feel concerned about the amount or severity of stress and problems they are experiencing with their adolescent are generally wise in seeking assistance fairly early, before things degenerate into a totally intolerable situation. Often, support is given through family counseling in which the whole family is involved. When the whole family is involved, many times problems and issues can be resolved rather quickly since there can be mutual understanding on everyone's part of what the problems are and mutual agreement as to how to proceed in handling them. However, support can also take the form of individual counseling for the adolescent. Such counseling can aid the young person in getting over developmental roadblocks and can therefore lower individual and family tension. Individual counseling can also help the adolescent deal more realistically with some of the peer influences he or she is most likely facing.

Parents need to know that much of the storm and stress of adolescence takes place during the period when the adolescent is in the twelve to fourteen age range. Many parents fearing the worst overreact. It is important that parents know that things are generally better by around age sixteen. Therefore, parents need to understand that changes are inevitable. Keeping in mind that there is a process taking place which for at least 80 percent of young people goes fairly well without intervention may also help parents weather the transition with a little more confidence.

5

Parents Are Changing, Too

One of the complexities for parents and young people is that children may enter adolescence at a time when many parents themselves may be feeling some upheaval. As we know, all life has different phases. One of the characteristics of the period of middle age (roughly, between the ages of thirty-five and sixty) is that it is a time of physical, mental, and emotional adjustment for adults—just as it is for adolescents. Some of the adjustments of middle age are diametrically opposed to those experienced by the adolescent, some are parallel but on a different dimension, and some actually are incongruous. These changes can muddy the interactions between parent and child if neither—parents, in particular—are aware of the possible reasons behind their attitudes and feelings.

For example, the physical changes that the adolescent experiences may be in direct contrast to changes the parent is experiencing. Physical changes may make the child taller or stronger than the parent. Merely the fact that the parent may no longer be able physically to control the child is an adjustment in itself; or a parent may *feel* less strong and able. Back problems or other injuries may actually make the parent less physically capable. Added body weight, the need for bifocals, and other signs of aging may contribute to the parent's feeling a waning sense of physical well-being, just as the child is gaining and expressing a new-found, enhanced physical self. There can be a subtle resentment on the part of parents, expressed as distaste for the adolescent's selection of clothing that reveals his or her maturing body; or the exact opposite: a vicarious push to have the child show off his or her body. Or there may be demands that young people take over heavier physical tasks, almost as punishment for having that capacity.

Young people during adolescence are becoming sexually more attractive. Their bodies fill out and they generally have a firmness and vitality that makes them very appealing. Their parents' bodies, on the other hand, may be becoming less attractive; the usual firmness and tone may be declining, wrinkles may begin showing. The body proportions may be changing despite their best efforts at diet and exercise. One mother wistfully commented: "I have the same measurements I did when I got married—it's just that everything is two inches lower." Parents may feel less sexually appealing just at a time when their child is becoming very sexually attractive.

Indeed, during middle age many men experience a concern about their virility; some may experience occasional impotence, which can create anxiety. Women, too, are changing. They are aware that their reproductive years may soon be over and some may be having menopausal symptoms. These experiences and feelings often contrast starkly with their child's heightened interest in sex and new reproductive capacity. Occasionally, parents may enter into competition with their children: A mother may try to look especially attractive to the daughter's boyfriend to prove she is still sexually appealing; fathers may flirt with their son's girlfriend.

During middle age, parents also experience subtle changes in how they relate to other people. Before this life phase, interactions with others frequently have had sexual currents: First impressions regularly included assessing the sexual attractiveness of the other person. Even continuing relationships of a supposed platonic or business nature often had sexual undertones. During middle age, as physical attractiveness declines and one anticipates a change in reproductive interest and capacity, this focus shifts. Parents may concentrate on relationships in a different way, and because of this their relationships with others can gain greater depth and meaning. This change, however, also creates a sexual-identity crisis. Particularly if parents have relied on their physical health and attractiveness as a way of confronting the world, it can create an upheaval. Because of this, relationships and reactions to their sexual adolescent can be distorted. Sorting out what such changes mean may make the parent restive and lacking in patience with children who are also trying to sort out the purpose, meaning, and importance of relationships in their lives.

Parents also reassess their relationships with the opposite sex. Parents who have divorced and not remarried may see the dating relationships of their child as reminders of experiences that did not work out well for them. Married parents during middle age often review their own marital status and partner choice. Parents who for years related to each other because of the child may suddenly find that, as the child moves on, they have little else in common and must reapply energies to getting to know one another again and finding mutual interests and activities. The sacrifice of their initial relationship for the children becomes painfully apparent to some, and such parents can resent their child's new love relationships when they feel they have lost much of the meaning in theirs.

Fathers may have some special problems. Many, who have for years focused much of their energies into achieving success in their careers, may have reached a point where they feel they can pull back a little and spend more time with their families. Turning their attention to the home just at a time when their child is distancing themselves from his or her parents in an attempt to become independent can be devastating. This is the time that the young person is much more anxious to be with peers than with parents, and increased demands for parent–child interrelationships at this time can set the stage for conflict and rebellion. If the young person has a boyfriend or girlfriend and an increased desire to spend additional time with that person, that relationship can become the symbol of the parent's frustration and the parent may resent or try to interfere in the relationship.

As parents proceed through middle age, and their own parents die, a final frustration can be the awareness of moving toward a less-valued life stage (old age) just as their child is moving into a highly regarded life stage (young adulthood). The parent may feel that their careers have peaked and that they have achieved as much as they are going to achieve, while the young person is just beginning to consider a wide variety of career choices. The parent may have some regrets about not having done certain things with his or her life just as the adolescent begins to talk about life as being open-ended and filled with opportunity. Also, the parent may want to rely on those values and actions that have stood him or her well for confronting life changes just at a time when the adolescent wants to challenge those values and actions in an attempt to sort out what he truly believes and the manner in which he wants to govern his actions.

All these events set the stage for further imbalance in relationships between parent and child just at a time when such relationships would normally experience at least some imbalance because of the child's passage through adolescence. Parents often report that they worry more about their children during adolescence than at any other time. Parents need to recognize that during this period they need to take some time for themselves. Changes are occuring within themselves that require some attention. Putting energy into handling personal adjustments and reaffirming their own flexibility in meeting life's challenges can ultimately aid parents in being able to more evenly support and guide their child throughout the adolescent's adjustment period.

6

Helping Adolescents
Manage Physical Feelings

Because young people develop the capacity and drive for physical intimacy before their psycho-social growth or experience can provide them with the skills they need to manage it, parents need to support and guide them in this area. Many studies show that significant portions of adolescents have engaged in intercourse, not because they wanted to, but because they felt their partner expected it of them and they didn't know how to refuse. Adolescents need help in examining what they see as expected behavior, understanding their rights in relationships, making decisions about physical expression, and developing skills to carry out their decisions, once made.

Examining Expected Behavior
Parents can help adolescents understand that there are a wide variety of ways that a person can show another person they care about them. On television or in the movies, if two people care about one another or are in love, most often they are shown expressing their feelings for one another through sexual intercourse; furthermore, expressing their feelings in that manner usually occurs very soon after the characters meet. The media also show people who are physically attracted to one another, but who are not nec-

essarily in love, becoming sexually involved. This modeling of casual sex influences teens' thinking about having sexual intercourse. One recent study showed that over half of all teens interviewed thought that the way sex and its consequences is shown on television is the way it is in real life. Many fewer adults felt that way.

Teens' attitudes about early sexual involvement have also changed. Many now feel that having sexual intercourse is just a part of growing up, just a part of a dating relationship. Peers mistakenly tell each other, "Everybody's doing it." This, like the media, sets a tone for sexual involvement.

Young teens often confuse the need for closeness, touch, and affection with "love." Being "in love" makes sexual involvement seem more permissible to teens. Parents should not deny that love and affection are often expressed in physical ways. However, parents need to point out that, in showing someone you care, more time and effort is generally spent in doing things that are non-physical, and that in lasting relationships it is the non-physical things that are remembered as the most important sign of caring. Parents can help young people think about the many ways that they can show someone they care for them without becoming sexually involved. Such ways need to be clearly explained as means of showing love and affection. For example, spending time listening to someone when he/she is upset and angry, without in turn getting upset or angry, can be a very loving thing to do.

Parents can also help young people understand the concept of love in broader terms than those shown by the media. Romantic attraction does not equal love: Such attraction may be based on physical attraction or attraction to the other person's personality. Love, on the other hand, is better described as a friendship that, over time, has deepened and grown into the kind of devotion that makes people feel committed to each other's well-being and happiness.

Learning to Handle Feelings

Learning to handle feelings regarding physical attraction and learning how to give, receive, and set limits on physical expressions of affection are important tasks for adolescents. Parents cannot ignore this area if they wish to be truly helpful to their teen. Indeed, it is important for parents to help adolescents understand why they need to think about the levels of expressing affection physically and decide on a stopping point. In particular, young people need to think about a stopping point in advance of engaging in such behavior. The time for teens to first think about what level they want to stop at is not when they are alone together and feeling very aroused.

Parents can also help teens understand that they need to be able to clearly communicate their decision to the person they are with. If that person doesn't agree, and continues to pressure them, or if the person does not respect their desire, then ultimately the teen should find someone whose beliefs and values are closer to his or her own.

Parents often feel uncomfortable about initiating a conversation around showing physical affection. Particularly if their child has just started dating, parents may worry that they might be suggesting behaviors the young person has not thought about or might find embarrassing. However, helping a young person think about such behaviors in advance is helping the young person to be prepared. It is important to remember that most youth are so unsure enough of themselves and what is expected of them that they don't like surprises. They like to know in advance, so that they can handle situations in ways that will support their ego and positive self-esteem. In helping them think through such situations, the parent therefore is meeting one of the real needs of their children.

One way to approach the subject is to talk about some basics people need to know when they start to date and how important it is to think through in advance how to handle certain kinds of situations that can occur after they have been dating for a while.

Use of the following diagram, taken from the educational series for youth called "Postponing Sexual Involvement," may be helpful to parents and young people.

Explaining Relationships

Introducing the topic of expressing affection physically within a relationship can be done in the context of a discussion about interpersonal relationships. Most young people are curious about relationships. Parents can explain that each person will meet many people over the course of a lifetime. Some will be viewed as acquaintances but never move beyond that point to become friends. Examples of such people are classmates, people met through after-school or summer jobs, etc. Later on, the same will be true of business acquaintances, people met in organizations belonged to or in one's neighborhood.

Someone may stand out, however, as a person the teen wants to get to know better. Over time, as the teen gets to know that person, a more special friendship may develop. The person becomes someone who can be trusted with ideas and feelings that are not always shared with others. Desires not to hurt each other but help each other may grow. Boys can have such relationships with boys, and girls can have them with girls. Such relationships are not just limited to boy–girl relationships.

If the relationship continues and if both people feel and act the same way in the relationship, it can become more meaningful. There can be a kind of dependency that develops, in which one sees the other person as someone to whom they can turn for comfort, advice, and support. There can develop a longing to be near the person and a safe secure feeling when one is with him or her. There can be a sharing of important secret thoughts and meaningful

SHOWING FEELINGS IN PHYSICAL WAYS

From "Postponing Sexual Involvement: An Educational Series for Young People," Emory University/Grady Hospital Teen Services Program, Grady Memorial Hospital, 80 Butler Street, S.E., Atlanta, Georgia 30335. Reprinted by permission.

emotions. For example, the teen may feel he or she can cry in front of that person and be understood, even when he or she feels it impossible to cry in front of anyone else.

As relationships mature, there may be a closeness and sharing that is expressed only with one special person, in several different ways. This kind of relationship generally occurs when the person is older; it is often described as an intimate relationship. It is important that young teens understand that people can have a meaningful—or even an intimate—relationship, and *not* have sexual intercourse. If the relationship is between a male and female, such a relationship can develop with someone to whom one is physically attracted, or a physical attraction can develop because of the depth of the relationship. Nevertheless, a physical relationship is not necessarily a part of an intimate relationship.

Teens generally feel both internal and external pressures to develop a relationship with a person of the opposite sex. Sometimes, teens date someone who is an acquaintance and going out together is used to decide if that is a person with whom one would really like to become friends. Most often, dates, however, are arranged with someone the teen feels already has moved beyond acquaintance to a beginning friendship.

For teens, one task of adolescence is to develop for the first time a meaningful close relationship with someone outside their own family. Many times teens choose someone of the opposite sex as the meaningful person. Parents often put down such relationships by describing them as "puppy love." Even when such a relationship ends, parents can unintentionally demean it by saying, "You'll get over it," or, "Don't worry. There'll be lots of other girls/boys." This belies the importance of the relationship to the young person and also overlooks the importance of the relationship as a precursor to the capacity for having a healthy adult relationship with someone of the opposite sex. Parents can empathize with the fact that breaking up often seems like the end of the world to the adolescent, at the same time remembering that adolescents are remarkably resilient and that they have amazing recuperative powers. The truly positive side is that with each relationship teens learn more about self and the kind of person who will be more compatible.

The more meaningful or intimate the relationship a teen has with another person, the more expressing affection physically may become a part of it. In talking over the diagram about expressing affection physically with their teens, parents will want to help teens understand that the first two upper steps may be shared with many people over their lifetime, but the middle and bottom steps are generally reserved for a small number of special people. With respect to the middle steps, there are probably not very many people with whom one would choose to relate in that manner. In most people's lifetime, the bottom step is shared with only a few people, In many people's lives, that step is reserved for just one very special person.

Once a young person has thought about an appropriate stopping point, he or she needs to be able to communicate that. Helping the young person develop the skills to say no can be a very important parental role. Most often, young people don't talk in advance about physical affection. As a couple move beyond kissing to caressing, communication begins only when an attempt is made to go beyond a certain point that one of them does not desire. Young people need to know that saying no can involve physical communication: removing a hand, moving away, pushing away, restraining. However, most physical communication needs to be reinforced by verbal communication. Parents can help young people by teaching them simple verbal assertiveness techniques for saying no.

Teaching Assertive Steps

The very first step in saying no is simply to *say no and keep repeating it.* It is important that parents tell their teen they don't have to make excuses or give a list of reasons. They can just say no:

"No, I don't want to do that."

"No. I don't *have* to tell you why. I can just tell you no."

"No. That's all there is to it. No!"

"I don't want to go any further. No."

"No. I've decided I don't wish to do that."

This strategy involves asserting one's rights. Most often, if the young person keeps saying no and says it firmly enough, the other person will accept his or her decision.

However, parents can also help the young person understand that occasionally there are people who are so self-concerned about getting what they want that they won't listen. In such a case, the parent can help the teen understand that another communication step can be taken. *The pressure can be turned around.* One way is to question the other person about the pressure:

"Why are you trying to make me do something after I've told you I don't want to do it?"

"Why do you keep pressuring me when I've told you no?"

"Don't you believe I have a right to decide for myself?"

"Don't you respect me enough to let me make my own decision?"

"But I've told you no. I'm not going to do that. Didn't you hear what I said?"

Another way is to turn the pressure around by telling the other person how their continued persistence makes the teen feel:

> "The fact that you keep pressuring me when I've told you no makes me angry with you."
> "The fact that you keep trying to make me do something I don't want to do makes me think you really don't care about me and just want to use me."
> "The fact that you keep trying after I've said no makes me wonder if I should go out with you again."

This strategy involves negotiating for mutual change. In all relationships there are conflicting desires and needs. Good relationships involve communication that makes it clear to the other person how one feels and how important the issue is to the person. Often, people truly interested in maintaining a good relationship will respond to such negotiation and stop the pressure.

If all else fails, however, young people need to know they have a right to *get out of the situation* by refusing to discuss the matter any more, or by physically removing themselves:

> "If you don't stop, I'm going to go inside the house."
> "Look, I'm not going to argue about this any more. I've said no and that's all there is to it."
> "Apparently you haven't heard what I've been saying. I'm leaving."
> "That's it. Now take me home."

This last strategy involves a demand for change. It is the strongest of the three strategies. Its very use signals that there is a problem in the relationship.

In talking about levels of expressing affection physically parents need to communicate that it is easy to get turned on so that even though one wants to stop, it becomes very difficult to do so. Parents should make it obvious, and important, that the young person should avoid putting themselves in situations where they *have* to stop, should try to avoid situations in which they *have* to say no.

The pressure to go further than the teen wants often comes from a boyfriend or a girlfriend. Because the teen may feel ambivalent about how to respond, it is important for parents to help teens acknowledge their ambivalence and that it is all right and normal to have such feelings. Knowing they have conflicted feelings, however, does not mean they have to act in the wrong manner. They can still say no:

> "Sure, I've wondered what it would be like, but I'm not going to do it."
> "If I was going to have sex with anyone, it would be with you—but I'm not going to do it."

Group Situations

Sometimes adolescents find themselves in group situations where others are becoming sexually involved. They may feel awkward or embarrassed and wish they could leave. They may wonder, however, if they leave whether they will ever be included again. There is tremendous group pressure at least to remain, if not to participate. Parents can convey to their teen that if they ever find themselves in that situation, they should simply leave. The temporary embarrassment of leaving is better than the increasing embarrassment of staying. Parents need to stress that the adolescent can always leave any situation that is uncomfortable, and that he or she doesn't owe anyone an explanation for doing so. One can just go.

Young people also need to know that their parents always will come and get them if they need them to do so. And they need to know that their parents will not question, chastise, or otherwise confront them. This is hard, sometimes, for parents to live with. A call may come at a most inconvenient time for a parent. But if an adolescent calls, wanting to be picked up, this may be one of the most supportive things a parent can ever do.

After picking up a teen, it can be difficult for a parent not to ask for a full explanation. However, a simple "Want to talk about it?" is probably the most supportive. If the answer is no, respect that. The adolescent may feel that, at a later point in time, they will want to talk. If they don't ever feel like talking, that's all right too. The fact that the young person called indicated that he or she had found a responsible way to handle an undesirable situation.

Some important concepts parents will want to share with their teen are:

- Teens' bodies are their own, and only they have the right to decide what they want to do with it.
- They do not owe anyone anything—pressure to become sexually involved, as payment, is using someone.
- They have a right to say no.
- No one has a right to pressure them into doing something they don't want to do; nor do they have a right to pressure others for the same purpose.
- They can just say no—they don't owe anyone an explanation.
- Many of the short-term needs teens try to meet through sexual involvement could be better met in other ways.

Helping teens feel good about themselves sexually, helping them greet awakening sexuality with the same healthy curiosity we expect of them in other areas is part of a parent's role. Equally important is the parent's role in helping adolescents acquire actual skills to use in managing their sexuality and sexual expression. Doing so can go a long way toward helping teens postpone sexual involvement.

7

Teens and Taking Risks

Risk-taking is a normal part of adolescent growth and development. Moreover, not all risk-taking behavior is dangerous or bad. Indeed, some risk-taking is absolutely necessary if young people are to grow to become mature, capable adults. A young man takes risks, for example, when he calls a girl on the telephone for the first time, gives a speech in front of the class, introduces himself to someone he doesn't know, eats a new food, begins to really care about someone who is not a member of his family.

Often young people engage in risk-taking behavior in an attempt to meet social or psychological needs, and most often adolescents are not aware of their underlying needs. When adolescents are asked about sexual risk-taking behavior, they make statements such as:

"We just got carried away."
"It was a dare."
"He wanted me to."
"I was so mad at my parents, I just did it to get back."
"I don't *know* why."
"Because of love."

One of the difficult tasks parents face is recognizing the difference between normal risk-taking behavior, which includes experimenting, and genuine problem behavior. Sometimes the difference is only in the degree and consistency of the behavior. Exploring another person's body or letting someone explore one's body is a different degree of experimentation from having sexual intercourse. Deciding to have sex once—to find out what it is like—is different from deciding that sex is just a normal part of a dating relationship.

However, one of the real problems is that having intercourse *just once* is a different degree of risk-taking from having a drink just once or having a cigarette once. A pregnancy or sexually transmitted infection can result from a single sexual experience, whereas such severe consequences are unlikely to flow from a limited one-time experience with the other traditional experimental youth behaviors. Parents therefore need to remind young people of the possible outcomes of sexual risk-taking behaviors as opposed to others.

Underlying Needs

To better understand risk-taking, it may be helpful to parents to be aware of some of the underlying needs that adolescents are trying to meet through such behavior; in particular, sexual behavior.

Adolescents have a need for feeling competent. They have a need for mastery. Feeling competent as a sexual human being is part of this overall need. Sometimes adolescents have sex to prove to themselves they can have and keep a boyfriend or girl friend. Adolescents thereby can meet a need for mastery too. Our society extolls the cool lover, the guy who's great in bed. No one wants to be really inexperienced, particularly young men. They have a need to feel, "I know what it's all about and I can do it well." Parents need to assist their adolescent in building a sense of mastery and competence in other areas of their life so that the sexual area does not become the primary pathway to meeting such needs.

Adolescents have a need to be accepted by their peers. If sexual behavior is engaged in by many of their peers, in particular by their closer friends, the desire to be like their peers may overwhelm their normal judgment about such behavior. Parents may need to try to help the adolescent find acceptable peers, whose values and beliefs are closer to their own. Parents also may need to help the young person avoid situations that would be conducive to sexual involvement. To provide guidance, parents need basic information such as knowing:

- where the couple is going
- how much time the couple will be spending together alone
- what kind of setting the couple will be in
- what kind of adult supervision there will be
- if it is a group situation, who the other people are who will be there
- what kinds of activities are planned
- where the couple will go afterward

Adolescents have a need for intimacy and physical closeness. As adolescents distance themselves from their families, they strive to establish new relationships outside that framework. In beginning to meet their needs outside the family context, inexperience often leads them to attach significance and meaning to new relationships that are really transient and superficial. Trying to meet their needs for intimacy and physical closeness in such relationships is often frustrating and disappointing. Mistakes can be made. Reassurance that those needs *can* be met in relationships, but that good relationships take time and waiting is not harmful but can be helpful to young people.

Adolescents have a need to test out physical capacities. They can desire to try out their maturing body in a number of ways. Some testing may involve feats of agility or physical strength. But their sexual drives propel young people forward toward testing their physical capacity in the sexual area. Some try out their capacity by making the body as attractive as possible to others. Girls do this through make-up, hairdos, clothes, and styles of walk or posture. Boys do it through clothes, hair styles, and manner of walking or posture as well. Young people also have a curiosity about what expressing affection physically feels like and would be like, including sexual intercourse. They may be anxious to test out their physical capacity in this manner. Parents need to help their boy, in particular, to be realistic about their feelings, as well as provide support for their son's managing sexual actions in a responsible manner.

Adolescents have a need for achievement of goals. Sometimes adolescents express this in the sexual area. They want to see how far the other person will go, and it becomes a game to see if they can get the other person to do something: "She'll do it for me if she really loves me." Boys with the goal of conquering girls sexually often will say and do dishonest or manipulative things they would not normally do. Parents need to have basic discussions about what it means to "use" someone and help their young people understand that using someone sexually is reprehensible behavior. Girls also "use" boys and sometimes will manipulate them through sexual interaction.

Handling Risk-Taking Behavior

In handling risk-taking behavior on the part of their young person, parents walk a difficult line. If parents overreact to light experimentation—take, say, an isolated incident and make an important event out of it—negative consequences can result. For example, if parents come home to find their daughter engaged in heavy caressing, accuse her of being promiscuous, or clamp down with severe punishment, the girl may rebel: "As long as they *think* I'm having sex, I might as well go ahead and have it. That way I won't have to take all this grief for nothing"; or: "All we were doing was necking. Next time, I'll really go far."

On the other hand, if a parent totally ignores that the teen is involved in such sexual behavior, the young person can be confused about what the acceptable limits are. When things are calmer, the parent will want to sit down and discuss the behavior and explain his or her own attitudes and expectations about such behavior.

Parents must therefore learn to balance their reactions appropriately between freedom and clear limits in order to aid the young adolescent in learning acceptable behaviors. In setting limits, parents must realize that their own orientation may not be shared by their teen. Adults bring a different perspective to control of behaviors than do adolescents. They have more life experience and have mastered cognitive skills and their application. Their values and moral development are matured. Adolescents, on the other hand, are usually inexperienced: They may just be beginning to think abstractly and to use logical reasoning skills; their moral development is still in the formative stage; they are caught up in the egocentrism of adolescence; their perspective is also different from that of their parents because they are trying to be independent and make their own decisions. Therefore, it is important that parents do not insist on certain limits for the sake of authority alone.

Young people need limits and rules that hold them responsible for their own behaviors. Rules should have logical, sound reasons. Although adolescents may not always agree with the logic, they can at least understand the reason for the rule. Rules and limits should be realistic and attainable. Even so, it is the rare adolescent who occasionally does not violate a rule or limit. When this happens, it is important that parents do not just look the other way or let the adolescent make excuses. Parents need to convey, when it happens, that failure to abide by the rule or limit on that occasion does not mean that the adolescent has shown he or she cannot live up to expectations but that, next time, he or she will need to think through how to do a better job.

As adolescents grow and mature, they will be able to accept more responsibility and want more independence. Some rules will be rules that the parents set up and will be "non-negotiable" throughout almost all adolescence: "Never ride in a car with an adolescent driver who has been drinking" is an example of a non-negotiable rule. Adolescents are more likely to follow non-negotiable rules if:

- the parent explains the reasons for the rules
- such rules are kept to a very few
- such rules are limited to those which, if violated, might bring serious harm to the adolescent or to another
- such rules relate to deeply held family values

In helping the adolescent balance between freedom and limits, parents should be very clear which rules are non-negotiable.

Negotiated Solutions

Other rules will be negotiable. Most often, negotiable rules center on tasks and behaviors parents think are important. Examples are: priority of homework over other activities, how late the adolescent may stay out, kinds and amounts of household chores the adolescent does. Such rules are made by parents and teens together, taking into account the needs of both. Participation in making such rules can help adolescents learn how to make decisions and assume responsibility for them. It is also a further step toward adulthood in that it integrates adolescents in a very clear way into the family decision-making. Negotiable rules are more open to change or "bending," as situations warrant.

Four common techniques parents have found to be helpful in discussing behaviors and negotiating solutions (rules) to guide behaviors are:

- Parents make clear statements about their feelings without being demeaning to their adolescent.
- Parents and their adolescent engage in thinking up solutions together.
- Parents and their adolescent listen to one another and sift through proposed solutions.
- Parents and their adolescent together agree which solution to adopt.

Making clear statements. Parents use these statements to convey feelings; they are not judgments, attacks, or putdowns. What these statements can do is allow the parents to talk about behavior or situations that are important— at least to the parent and perhaps to the young person.

"I worry when you go over to Rick's house when his parents aren't home."

"I worry that spending so much time together could lead to situations in which either one or both of you would not want to or not be able to stop from going all the way."

Young people can make clear statements about feelings too:

> "I feel like you don't trust me. You know I wouldn't do anything like that."

Parents can make clear statements in response:

> "It's frustrating for me when you think that trust is the issue. I know you wouldn't *intend* to do something. The issue is really being alone together for a long time, where you might be tempted to do things you would not ordinarily do."

Thinking up solutions. Parents try to come up with ways to handle the defined issue, and encourage their adolescent to do the same.

> "Perhaps we could agree upon times or places when it is O.K. for you and Rick to be alone together, and also for when it is not."
> "One solution could be that when Rick's parents aren't home, you go someplace where the two of you could be alone but be in a public spot."
> "Another solution might be to agree that when Rick's parents aren't home, you and Rick come here as long as I'm (we're) home."

Sifting through solutions. As they discuss the problem and possible solutions, parents need to listen not only to what the adolescent has to say but the feelings that go along with the statements. If parents listen and communicate back what has been heard, the adolescent will be able to see himself/herself more clearly. The adolescent will understand that the parents really do want to understand how they think and feel. Parents will also be enabled to better understand what the adolescent is saying. Finally, the parent will be modeling some important skills about communication that the adolescent can use throughout his/her life.

> "I don't see why people always have to be spying on Rick and me."
>
> "It sounds like what you really want with Rick is some privacy."
>
> "Yes, and whenever Rick and I come here, my brother is always hanging around spying on us."

Agreeing together on a solution. Parents and teens try to agree on a solution that is acceptable to both, or that is at least one the parents can live with.

> "Well, I think your brother hangs around because Rick is a big deal to him. He really looks up to him. However, that is neither here nor there, if it bothers you. A solution might be to agree that when Rick's parents aren't home, you and Rick come here and I'll see to it that your brother stays out of the den when you two are here. Do you think setting a rule like that would be worth a try?"
>
> "Well, we could try it, but the first time my brother comes sneaking around, the deal's off."

Keep Dialogues Going

Negotiating solutions to problems is not always an easy process. Teens may sometimes be confrontal in conversations. Since they need to rebel to become independent, they cannot always constructively enter into dialogues. Parents sometimes get so hostile in response that the attempts to communicate degenerate into arguments and fights. This can intensify conflict or distress unproductively. Hard-to-handle situations can result.

Some techniques to defuse explosive situations are:

Paraphrasing. Paraphrasing the teen's remark can have the effect of letting him or her know you have heard the comment but can also soften it to be less hostile or confrontal.

> "I'm going to see Peter as much as I want, and you can't stop me."
> "Are you saying that seeing Peter more often is important enough to you to take the consequences that would come from breaking the rule about no dating on weeknights?"

Partially agreeing. Partially agreeing with the teen's remark can defuse the issue by agreeing that there is some merit to the point of view being presented. Such acknowledgment can reduce the level of confrontation. For example, a parent could say:

> "You do have a point about it being difficult to stop you."

The parent could leave it there, waiting for the adolescent to speak again. Or the parent could say:

> "You do have a point about it being difficult to stop you. However, the real issue is dating on week nights, when we agreed that during the school year you would date only on weekends."

Waiting to respond. Waiting to respond is another way to defuse the situation. Waiting gives both parent and child time to cool off, think, and come up with a response to the issue that is better thought through and less confrontational.

> "I'd like to think about weeknight dating some more before I answer."

During any discussion it is important for parents to remember that sometimes the *way* they say things can do as much, or more, to defuse an issue as *what* they say. A sarcastic, angry tone can escalate a discussion while a calm quiet tone can ease tension. It is rare that disagreements or confrontations are resolved satisfactorily when people are shouting at each other. If parents can try to show teens the same interest and courtesy they would show their adult friends, it can make a positive difference in parent–teen discussions.

Negotiating with teens can further young people's ability to make responsible decisions and follow through on them. Parents also can learn to "let go" in positive ways. The process is not always easy, but it is another step toward the goal of helping adolescents achieve maturity and independence.

8

Adolescent Feelings and Emotions

O ne of the difficulties that get in the way of parents' and adolescents' communicating is the bewildering variety of new feelings and emotions that the adolescent is experiencing. Often, things are more intensely experienced in adolescence than at any other time of life. Sometimes adolescents have difficulty identifying what their true emotions are. For example, an adolescent girl may be expressing anger at a parent when, inside, she is really feeling another emotion. "I hate you. Why did you let my friends in without telling me?" may be what the adolescent is saying while, inside, the feeling she identifies as hate toward the parent is really one of embarrassment of self over having walked into the living room in a bathrobe and hair curlers. One of the tasks of adolescence is learning to recognize and cope with one's true feelings.

Coping with Feelings Through Learning New Skills

Knowing true feelings is important because, if teens know clearly what their real feelings are, they can make better decisions about them. Parents can help teens cope with negative emotions and the situations that cause them by teaching them some ways of handling them.

Sticking with it. Sometimes teen-agers try to run away from their feelings, only to make them worse. Parents can therefore help their teen "stick with it." If teens can learn to accept their uneasiness with their emotions and do the best they can with the situation that is causing them to feel so uncomfortable, it will strengthen them. Living through difficult situations can be a tremendous learning experience for teens and can help show them that no matter how bad they think something is, they can survive it.

When relationships end, for example, teens often feel they can't face the other person. However, that person may be someone they go to school with and is therefore a person they will see in the halls, in classes, or at school activities. Dealing with the feelings they have when they see the person, although painful, in the long run may be positive. Later on, they can look back on that time and learn from it.

Escaping. On the other hand, parents can also help their teen understand that sometimes the best thing to do is just the opposite: Rather than sticking with it, "escape from it." Sometimes situations arise that are not readily resolved, and dwelling on the situation and the emotions it creates is not healthy. Getting a little distance by turning attention away and allowing room for other feelings can be the best approach. Later, the teen may be able to be more objective about the problem and handle it better. Sometimes the best way to get away from a problem is to get involved with something else that requires both time and energy.

Using fantasy. This is another technique that can be helpful in dealing with emotions that arise from problem situations. Adolescence is normally a time of fantasy. Fantasies are very good for adolescents because they allow adolescents to try themselves out in situations without actually having to experience them. Even in real situations, however, fantasies can be very useful in that adolescents can take the time mentally to draw on all their resources and problem-solve in a variety of ways—before taking action.

Redefining the situation.　This is another way of helping deal with negative emotions. Certain situations can bring on a wide variety of conflicting or confusing emotions. Therefore, if parents show teens how to separate out the various issues and the emotions that flow from each, it can be helpful. For example, a teen whose boyfriend has wanted her to go further sexually than she wants to go can be very upset if he takes out another girl who, she thinks, may be more likely to give in to his wishes. Helping her keep separate the issues of what her own values and feelings are about sexual involvement and the issue of her boyfriend dating another girl can keep her from letting her conflicting emotions lead her to do something she really does not wish to do.

Facing the problem squarely.　This is another way teens can be helped to handle emotions. Allowing things to drag on can be a drain on emotional strength. For this reason, deciding that the situation needs to be met head-on and dealt with is a strategy parents can help teens learn. Once teens are able to handle a problem in this manner, they learn that they can control even difficult situations by dispatching them promptly. Being quickly freed to go on to more positive situations and feelings is a more-than-adequate reward.

Using others constructively.　This is another technique that parents can teach young people. Sometimes handling problems, and the negative emotions that flow from them, is just too big a job for adolescents to handle all by themselves. Parents can role-model how they involve others in helping solve their own problems. They can also make it clear to the adolescent that they are available to help. Finally, they can reassure the adolescent that turning to others is a sign of maturity, and that they will not be upset if they, themselves, are not the ones to whom the adolescent turns.

For the parent, the test comes in sharing these strategies with the adolescent without confusing what may be normal healthy responses to a situation that will in time dissipate with unhealthy responses that need action to resolve. For the adolescent, the test comes in figuring out which strategy, if any, is appropriate to use in which situation. Parents can be supportive by discussing the various alternatives to handling problems and emotions stemming from them, in advance of the problem situations' arising. That way, adolescents can be helped to bring some objectivity to whatever situation does arise. It will not be completely new to them at a time when they are feeling bad. Ultimately, this will enable the adolescents to better understand the choice they are making and be more confident in learning from the outcome.

Other Techniques

Another way parents can assist teens with negative feelings is to help them identify ways of "talking back" to these. Parents are sometimes not aware of how hard teens are on themselves. Teens are constantly judging themselves and doing internal talking: "Boy, am I stupid! Why did I act like such a jerk?" Such self-talk often makes it hard for teens to control their emotions and feelings, because they exacerbate them with negative thoughts. Here is an example:

Situation:
   "My boyfriend insisted on staying for the end of the baseball game, even though it went into extra innings. I was bored with it so I picked a fight and left."

Negative Thought:
"I'm really a horrid person. It's amazing he continues to go out with me."
Follow-through feelings:
Depression, anxiety
Thoughts about next behavior:
"I better try to please him when I see him again or he might drop me. Maybe I'll go a little farther sexually."

Teens can be taught, instead, to react with more helpful thinking.

Positive thought:
"I'm not grouchy very often. I'll try not to do that again."
Follow-through feelings:
Pleasant anticipation, relief
Thoughts about next behavior:
"I'll sit through the whole baseball game with him, next time. However, I'll tell him if it goes into extra innings and we stay, we have to go again together to see that movie I thought was so great."

In particular, stress among young people often brings on negative thoughts. Such thoughts are comments such as all people make to themselves about their own conduct. And such comments directly affect feeling and behavior. Comments can sometimes be helpful. The adolescent needs to learn to tell the difference between the helpful comments and the non-helpful comments. In what is sometimes referred to as "self-talk," parents can help young people learn how to use talking to oneself in constructive ways.

Young people will sometimes verbalize their negative thoughts, giving parents evidence they may need help in this area. Parents can help their teen identify negative thoughts and replace them with positive ones. Often, *imagining* a situation in which a person has to think positively to help him- or herself out helps the young person get involved in the process.

The parent can think up a situation and give a negative thought about it, and let the young person think up the positive-response thought.

Negative: "The kids all would think I'm a dork if they knew I hadn't had sex yet."

Positive: "Now, wait a minute! I'm still the same person whether I've had sex or not."

Negative: "But we'd have that in common. I'll feel out of it if they find out I haven't done it, when they have."

Positive: "Even if a lot of my friends have done it, there are other people who haven't. Besides, I have other things in common with my friends."

Negative: "You won't really fit with your friends unless you do it. You'll wind up being all alone and left out."

Positive: "I don't have to do everything my friends do. If they really are my friends, they'll respect my rights in this area. Plus, I'll meet new kids when I go to high school next year, so I can gradually try to add new friends and maybe not spend quite as much time with my old friends."

Anxiety and depression are two powerful feelings that can also be dangerous to a young person's health and functioning. Young people who are most at risk for anxiety and depression are those who have low self-esteem, a sense of loneliness, or a feeling that life is out of control. Parents should try to help them improve their sense of control and their own ability to pull themselves up. Such young people may need help in learning how to solve problems on their own. Parents can teach young people this skill in general terms and then show them how to apply it to specific issues.

Problem-solving

The first step in problem-solving that parents can help the adolescent learn is identifying what the problem is: "The guys are always bugging me, saying I must be gay because I haven't had sex with my girl friend yet." The next step is showing the adolescent how the problem could be made concrete and turned into a positive goal: "I'd at least like my best friend Mike to understand I can be just as much a man without having sex with my girlfriend." The adolescent can be helped to think of alternative ways of solving the problem.

> "Get Mike to understand that I respect Cindy too much to pressure her into doing something she doesn't want to do."
> "Get Mike to understand that having sex with Cindy just to prove something to him and the other guys is using her, and I don't like using people."
> "Get Mike to talk about other ideas he has about what makes a man a man, so that he doesn't keep bugging me about sex as the only way."
> "Stop having Mike as my best friend and try to find someone who will respect me and not try to push me into doing something I don't want to do."

Weigh the pros and cons of each alternative and make them more concrete:

> "Invite Mike to my house without the other guys and just sit and talk to him about what he thinks makes a

man, and then tell him to get off my back about sex being the only way."

The parent can then share with the adolescent the remaining steps of picking the alternative that seems best, deciding how the solution will be carried out, and then acting on it. After the outcome has become clear, if the solution worked well the parent can praise the adolescent, letting him or her take credit for having solved the problem. If the solution didn't work as well as had been hoped, the parent can enable the adolescent to take credit for having gone through the process and having tried to solve it. The parent can support the adolescent in *analyzing* what was learned from having gone through the process. If the problem is still one that needs solving, the parent then can support the adolescent while they define the problem again and repeat the process.

Adolescent Feelings as Reflections of Parent Behavior

Sometimes adolescents have difficulty in problem-solving and become stressed and rebel because of parental behavior that is not constructive. Parents, in their desire to help their child achieve and do well, may be unnecessarily critical and may constantly give unwanted advice.

Often such critical behavior is unconscious. The parent who looks at the child's report card and sees no As but instead all Bs may say, "Don't worry, you'll do better next time. But even if the child, too, is disappointed in those grades, the statement is really not the supportive one the parent intended. There is an implied criticism, implied failure. A supportive statement might have been: "You've obviously done consistently good work in your classes this time. I think you should take pride in that." In much the same manner, the parent who tries to console the young person who wasn't invited to a party being held by the "popular kids" may unconciously make the young person feel worse and more desperate to be accepted by a certain group. Parents must be careful, therefore, how their own attitudes toward popularity might undercut young people's confidence.

Many times, parents constantly give unwanted advice that makes the young person feel he or she can't solve problems on his or her own. For example: "I think you should limit the number of kids you invite to your party so you'll be sure to have enough room for dancing." Parents need to understand that when young people are doing just fine, constantly giving advice undermines their self-confidence and sense of independence. Even if the advice is sound and the young person takes it, he or she may feel that the parent always gets his/her way, always runs things, always makes the decision— "so why should I try to be responsible?"

Some young people respond to unwanted advice by listening, not saying anything, and then by going ahead and doing what they want to do. The parent then feels, "Sally never listens to what I say." Or the parent says, "I told you before you had the party that you should limit the number of kids so there'd be room for dancing. That's probably why they started doing all that necking and petting—because there wasn't room." Neither the parental feelings nor attitudes are helpful, and so the situation is likely to be repeated.

Rather than give outright advice, the parent might have asked, "What do you think makes a really successful party?" Or: "What kinds of things have you most enjoyed at the parties you've been to? Are you planning any of those things for your party?" Or: "How important was the amount of dancing space they had at those parties?" Or the parent can initiate a discussion of the ways the young person could ask for advice or the parent could give advice that would be mutually satisfying.

Parents who are so anxious to help their child avoid embarrassing situations, problem situations, or mistakes that they constantly "take over," with unsolicited advice or direction, are not being helpful. Unless the results of non-intervention can have serious long-term negative consequences, the parent is better off not intervening, and letting the young person seek advice as needed. The parent can still make a supportive statement such as, "If you need or want any help about your party, just let me know." However, the overall thrust should be to let the young people know that you respect their ability and judgment to carry out the task. Young people who gain experience in making decisions, carrying them out, and living with the consequences are much more likely to learn when to ask for advice and when to trust their own abilities than those who don't have such opportunities. Teens learn from their mistakes as well as from their successes.

For example, one outcome of a young person's experience in not having enough dancing space might be that he or she says, "Janet's invited me to her party, but she doesn't plan on any dancing at all. I know what happened at my party. When the kids couldn't dance, they all ended up necking. I'm not sure I want to go to her party if that's all they're going to do."

Parents are constantly faced with the delicate balance between intervention and non-intervention. However, when the young person seems abnormally stressed or depressed, the parents may feel a real need to intervene.

How to Help the Teen Who Feels "Down"

Parents need to know that depression and stress can be reduced, in part, by physical exercise. When people are depressed or stressed, often they feel they haven't got the energy to do anything. Physical activity can actually counteract that "drained" feeling that depressed people experience and increase their feelings of having new energy. Physical activity can mean dancing, skating, taking walks, doing aerobics. Sometimes depressed adolescents simply can't think of anything to do, and resist doing anything. It may take some parental pushing to get them out and exercising.

Parents can also help young people understand that to help avoid feeling depressed or to pull themselves out of such a feeling, they must structure some pleasure into their lives. When they are not depressed, they should make a list of the things they like to do as reminders for themselves. Even if the pleasurable activity only pulls them out of their depression for an hour or so, it gives them a little relief and models the power they can have over dealing with their feelings. Pleasurable activities may be sitting outside just watching cloud formations, listening to music, going someplace just to window-shop. Generally, pleasurable activities are things all people enjoy. Again, however, parents may need to push young people who are depressed into picking something on their list and doing it.

Finally, parents can encourage young people to take pride in small accomplishments and, if possible, reward themselves for them. Stress and depression often leave the young person unable to appreciate on almost every level their positive functioning. Stress or depression are often related to unrealistic expectations. Parents can help young people realize how much they are doing well and not take such achievements for granted. Often the things young people neglect taking pride in are schoolwork, personal grooming, household chores, and family interactions. For example, young persons should be encouraged to be proud of getting to school on time, washing their hair, saying something nice to a sibling, keeping the laundry picked up off the floor and put in the laundry barrel, finishing their homework. And they should be encouraged to reward themselves: "Since I got up and got to school on time every day this week, I'm going to sleep late an extra hour on Sunday." Or: "As soon as I finish straightening up my room, before I do anything else I'm going to reward myself by watching a movie on the VCR."

And parents need to help their young people set some realistic goals. Having something to work toward, to look forward to, can help young people better see the merit in coping with current stress including the pressures to become sexually involved.

Parents can give additional support for coping with stress and depression, or the wide variety of other conflicts and problems adolescents face, by helping young people see the natural "people resources" that exist in their environments. Young people need to know that parents will not feel offended if the young person turns to others for advice, counsel, cheering up, or special supports.

Young people can be helped to identify who those people are and what they can offer. Youth leaders, ministers, teachers, family friends, neighbors, and relatives can generally play some helpful role. Being able to call up favorite understanding relatives and talk over problems with them—including one's problems with parents—can go a long way toward alleviating stress. Sometimes just getting things out in the open and having the teen express how he or she feels about the problem can put the teen on a path toward resolving it. Certainly, having people to turn to to help cope with the stress of social and peer sexual pressures, as well as the depression that can result when young people feel their male–female relationships aren't going well, can go a long way toward helping postpone sexual involvement.

Parents should never hesitate to seek out counseling help

for themselves or their adolescent if it seems warranted. Young people who are very depressed or stressed can be tempted to engage in sexual behavior they might not normally consider. Later on, when they are feeling in better balance, they may regret some of the decisions they made.

9

Today's Sexual Society and Teens

Young women and young men throughout time have generally become sexually involved around the age of puberty unless there were strong societal constraints. Adults who grew up in a different time realize that societal constraints have lessened greatly in the last few decades as sexual values and mores have changed.

The Social Climate

The social climate of today's society is one in which sexuality is deeply ingrained. Our society uses sex—on TV, in the movies, in songs—as public entertainment and as a source of humor. Clothing is often designed to exhibit body shape and emphasize sexual anatomy. Some clothing even is lettered with sexual messages (T-shirts that say, "Squeeze Here" or "This Side Up for Rape"; hats that say, "World's Greatest Lover"). Cars are decorated with sexual messages (bumper stickers that say "Divers Do It Deeper," Backpackers Do It Anywhere," "Librarians Are Novel Lovers") and sexual messages are on our greeting cards and souvenirs. All these serve to keep sexual images on the mind.

Sex is also used to sell products. Young people will see over 500,000 advertisements by the time they graduate from high school. Sexual messages are a common advertising ploy, intertwining images of the good life, physically attractive youth, and sexual behavior. Most often, advertisements portray sexual situations in which sex is without commitment and without consequences.

By the time they graduate from high school, young people will have spent more hours in front of a television set than in school classrooms. Often the sexual messages from the media—TV in particular, but also radio, movies, magazines, records, and performing groups—end up creating distorted images of reality for young people.

On television, the characters meet someone in the first few minutes of a program, then become physically involved within the next few minutes. Not only do time and events become encapsulated on television but use of time is distorted. In reality, people have much more to do with their lives than just become sexually involved. In real life people do time-consuming things such as getting their cars serviced; they have to solve how to get their car to the service shop, how to get to work without their car, how to get back to the service shop to pick it up at the end of the day. On television, people never do the common things that take time in real life, thus giving unreal impressions of the amount of time adults spend on sexual involvement—and of its preeminence over other activities. This also belies the fact that good relationships take time.

Images of men and women are often distorted too. Many qualities of both males and females in real life are ignored in favor of sexual interests and prowess. In afternoon television programs there are over two sex acts or innuendos per hour. On evening television there is at least one such act or innuendo per hour. And sexual involvement, as it is presented on television, is often hostile or manipulative sex. (For example, a woman sleeps with someone to get his vineyards.) Further, 94 percent of the sexual behavior on television is among people who are not married to one another—even if a character is married, he or she is shown generally in sexual situations with someone other than the spouse. Clearly this sends the message to young people that marital sex is not interesting or "good" sex.

However, it is not just the changes in media images and messages that influence teen thinking. Changes in actual adult behaviors influence young people too. In today's society, young adults as well as older adults often live together before marriage. Sexual relations are also more common in the life-styles of divorced parents. The sexual aspects of the lives of prominent adults also have become more common knowledge. What used to be rumor is now often made fact by investigation and indiscriminate publicity.

It is therefore important that parents help their adolescent distinguish the difference in behavior that is appropriate for adults and adolescents. Unfortunately, young people learn more by what we *do* than what we *say*, and their desire to be and act adult muddies the waters. Parents who are single and dating have special issues to worry about; young teens may go to spend the weekend with their divorced father and find that his girlfriend may be staying the weekend also. Issues about behavior can be raised that are not easily resolved.

Life-Style Changes

However, in addition to behavioral changes among adults in our society, life-style changes also have an impact. There are more temptations for teens. In today's world, help is no longer needed at home, in the family business, on the farm. Machines now wash and dry clothes, compact the trash, so that young people have much more free time.

Further, neighborhoods tend to be less stable. The average American family moves every three or four years. Many young people grow up in areas where their neighbors are not really known to them. Porches with people sitting on them have been replaced by privacy and locked doors. Moreover, the sense of community that children once experienced has changed. While, at one time, neighbors took an interest in children and felt they had some rights to help guide and shape the youth around them, this is no longer true. Neighbors no longer offer friendly guidance and support, nor do they scold. At one time, if a boy and girl went into a house or apartment when the parents were known not to be home, it would have been noticed by neighbors and quickly reported to a relative or the parents; or the neighbor might have confronted the young people directly. This is no longer the case.

Working patterns, as well as the entertainment and personal-growth activities of many families, mean that many adolescents are left at home or outside in unsupervised situations. Single-parent homes, two working parents, parents busy with personal interests or in meeting the needs of other children all contribute to the fact that there really are not very many people around youth today.

What this lack of parental supervision, lack of relative supervision, lack of neighborhood supervision of teen activities means is a reduction in the numbers and kinds of support for the young person's own internal limit-setting. It is therefore not surprising that the majority of girls who become pregnant in the United States do so in their own homes. The opportunity to be alone in a comfortable setting where they feel in charge is too great a temptation for many young people. Babysitting provides another tempting setting for some young people. In a home where young children are often put to bed, and adults specify the time period they will be gone, girls who have their boyfriends over to keep them company are left solely to their own resources to make decisions.

So teens are confronted with having to act independently more often. There are not the surrounding support mechanisms there once were. And the pressures toward sexual involvement have increased. The degree to which social pressures now influence young people's attitudes and values is shown in the following chart, as reprinted in the "Let's Talk" materials in Atlanta, Georgia.

ESTIMATED SHIFTS IN THE INFLUENCES UPON 13–19-YEAR-OLDS WHICH CHANGE THEIR VALUES AND BEHAVIOR*

	1960		1980		
1st	Mother, Father	1st	Friends, Peers	(Up	2)
2nd	Teachers	2nd	Mother, Father	(DOWN	1)
3rd	Friends, Peers	3rd	Television, Radio, Records, Cinema	(UP	5)
4th	Ministers, Priests, Rabbis	4th	Teachers	(DOWN	2)
5th	Youth club leaders, Counselors, Advisers, Scoutmasters, Coaches, Librarians	5th	Popular Heroes, Idols in sports, music	(UP	1)
6th	Popular Heroes, Idols in sports, music	6th	Ministers, Priests, Rabbis	(DOWN	2)
7th	Grandparents, Uncles, Aunts	7th	Newspapers, Magazines	(UP	2)
8th	Television, Records, Cinema, Radio	8th	Advertising	(UP	2)
9th	Magazines, Newspapers	9th	Youth club leaders, Counselors, Advisers, Scoutmasters, Coaches, Librarians	(DOWN	4)
10th	Advertising	10th	Grandparents, Uncles, Aunts	(DOWN	3)

*Johnston Company synthesis of eighteen studies for youth and values-oriented clients 1954–1980.

From "Let's Talk: Campaign for Responsible Parenthood." Emory University/ Grady Hospital Teen Services Program, Grady Memorial Hospital, 80 Butler Street, S.E., Atlanta, Georgia 30335. Reprinted by permission.

The chart also indicates the degree of change in the importance of peer pressures upon teen decision-making. The teen years represent a time of change, a movement away from childhood toward adulthood. As they seek independence and self-identity, teens often experiment, defy authority, and try to impress their peer group. With social and peer influence so strong, young people become vulnerable to pressures from these sources toward sexual involvement.

Pressures That Lead Teens to Sexual Involvement

Sometimes pressures on young people to become sexually involved come from peer attitudes about virginity. Direct observations by friends—"Hey, girl! What's the matter with you, anyway? All your friends are doing it" or "He's never had a girl. He's still mama's little boy"—are hard for teens to cope with. One of the things parents can do is help young people understand that bragging about sexual exploits can be a hurtful, even harmful thing to do. Parents also need to understand, however, that young people often get tired about being kidded about not having sex and may need other supports. Adolescents can get worn down. Teens sometimes say, "I finally just did it so I could say I'd done it."

Pressures to be accepted, to be one of the crowd, are also difficult for young people to handle. If the young person's friends actually are having sex, or if the young person thinks they are having sex even though they aren't, it can make him or her more vulnerable.

Another pressure that teens sometimes use with one another involves playing on the person's natural curiosity about sex. "Don't you want to try it and see what it's like?"

they will ask. An equally strong pressure can come from creating the notion that all young people are sexually involved: "Oh, c'mon. Everybody's doing it."

Teens also try to create a sense of guilt or obligation on the part of the other person: "Look, I spent a lot of money on you. I took you to a rock concert and took you out afterwards. You owe me something in return." In our "payback" society, inexperienced young people can be confused about what their obligation really is and how to handle such a situation.

Teens can also threaten each other. One powerful threat teens sometimes use on one another is the loss of their relationship. "If you don't want to have sex with me, then I don't want to see you anymore." Or: "Look, if you don't have sex with me, then somebody else will."

Another pressure comes from societal messages that being sexually free is being liberated. Parents need to counteract these messages by helping young people understand that being liberated means that women have the right to control their own lives and to make their own decisions—but they still must be responsible for their actions. Being sexually involved is a very personal decision that requires a mature attitude and ability to resist pressures to do things that are not personally appropriate.

Still another pressure comes from the fact that young boys and even adult men often have a genuine discomfort or fear about homosexuality. Because of that, one of the more devastating insults a young man can hear is that he is "gay." Boys tend to kid each other or pressure each other by saying that if a particular teen is not having sex, he must be a homosexual. If a young man is still virginal, he can be hurt and feel some internal doubt; it can make him feel he is less a person than he should be. Certainly, helping young people understand what makes a man can be helpful. Being a man means standing up for your own beliefs, making and carrying out your own decisions. Having sex with a female does not make a man a real man.

Sometimes pressures to become sexually involved come from young people deciding that having sex will make them grown-ups. Young people have a strong desire to be independent, to make their own decisions and guide their own behaviors. However, should a pregnancy occur, few adolescents could fully bear the responsibility for such consequences to their actions. Parents should make certain young people know that one sure sign of adulthood is waiting until they can assume full responsibility for the consequences of their actions before engaging in certain behaviors.

Sometimes a pressure to become sexually involved results when teens feel their parents are being too strict. Since teens want to appear like adults and to be independent from their parents, too many restrictions create special pressures on teens to show that they are not just children. Some teens use sexual involvement as a way of defying their family's wishes about sexual restraint: "My parents don't have any control over where I go and what I do." Some teens use sexual involvement as a way of getting back at their parents for some real or imagined hurt: "They'd die if they knew I was having sex." Parents who criticize their children or warn them through put-downs can also create a self-fulfilling prophecy: "My mom always told me I was no good and I'd probably end up getting pregnant—and see, I did!"

Preparing Teens to Handle Pressures

Part of adolescence is facing new desires, opportunities, decisions, and expectations with limited life experience upon which to base decisions. Parents can help their children be more prepared to deal with pressures by making them aware of the strategies that their peers use in trying to make them do something they don't want to do or something not in their best interests to do. Parents can also help their teens be prepared to respond to such strategies and pressures.

Going over with teens the "lines" that some teens use to try to pressure others into doing things, and helping them think up their own responses to such "lines," can be helpful. The following are some useful examples.

Pressure "Lines" and Assertive Responses *

1. *Line:* "Everybody's doing it."
   Reply: "Well, I'm not everybody, I'm me. Besides, I don't really believe everybody is doing it. I think it's a lot of talk."

2. *Line:* "If you love me you'll have sex with me."
   Reply: "If you love me, you'll respect my feelings and not push me into doing something I'm not ready for."

3. *Line:* "If you won't have sex with me, then I don't want to see you anymore."
   Reply: "Well if that's the way you feel, I'm going to miss seeing you. But that's the way it's got to be."

4. *Line:* "I know you want to do it. You're just afraid of what people will say."
   Reply: "If I wanted to do it, I wouldn't be arguing with you about it."

5. *Line:* "It's just part of growing up."
   Reply: "Having sex doesn't mean you're grown-up. Being grown-up to me means deciding what I believe and then sticking to those beliefs."

*From "Postponing Sexual Involvement: An Educational Series for Young People," Emory University/Grady Hospital Teen Services Program, Grady Memorial Hospital, 80 Butler Street, S. E., Atlanta, Georgia 30335. Reprinted by permission.

6. *Line:* "I want to marry you someday."

   Reply: "Marriage is a long way off for me. There's lots I want to do and see. I want to wait until I'm older to have sex."

7. *Line:* "We had sex once before, so what's the problem now?"

   Reply: "I have a right to change my mind. I've decided to wait until I'm older."

8. *Line:* "You don't want people to think you're not a man (woman)."

   Reply: "Having sex doesn't prove you are a man (woman). It's not for me right now."

9. *Line:* "Don't you want to try it to see what it's like?"

   Reply: "I think that's a pretty poor reason to have sex—pretending to care just so you can see what it's like. No thanks!"

10. *Line:* "But I have to have it!"

    Reply: "No you don't. If *I* can wait, *you* can wait."

11. *Line:* "If you want to be popular with the kids at school, you'll do it."

    Reply: "I don't have to depend on sex to be popular. I have more to offer than that. People like you because of the kind of person you are, the kind of character you have."

12. *Line:* "If you get pregnant, I'll marry you."

    Reply: "I don't want to risk getting pregnant, and I'm not ready to get married."

13. *Line:* "You want it as much as I do."

    Reply: "No, I really don't. I've got a lot of plans for my life and I don't want to mess things up by getting pregnant (getting you pregnant)."

14. *Line:* "You've got me all excited. If you love me, you'll prove it."

    Reply: "Having sex doesn't prove you're in love. I have too much self-respect to get sexually involved before I'm ready for it. I've decided to wait."

15. *Line:* "Hey, let's find out about the fireworks they're always talking about on TV and in the movies."

    Reply: "TV and the movies are just shows, a make-believe world—not the way life really is. 'Fireworks' like that don't usually happen, except maybe when you have invested a lot of time with another person and care deeply for that person."

16. *Line:* "Come on, take a drink. It will get you in the mood."

    Reply: "No thanks, I don't want to get drunk and not know what I'm doing."

17. *Line:* "If *you* don't, someone else will."

    Reply: "If all I mean to you is a body to have sex with, maybe we'd better take a closer look at why we see each other. You have no right to use me."

18. *Line:* "A lot of your friends are doing it. You're just not with it."

    Reply: "What my friends decide to do is their business. I make my own decisions. What may be right for my friends isn't necessarily right for me. I've decided to wait. That's my decision."

The Importance of Parental Values

Some parents firmly believe that sex should be performed only within a marital context. Certainly they will want to convey that to their young person. However, the influences of the society are strong. We live in a society, one study indicated, in which one half of American women believe premarital sex is a sin and the other half do not. That means that through family, friends, and social messages, young people are likely to be exposed to other values that state that it is not important to wait until marriage.

If parents are only concerned about consequences—that is, they convey to the adolescent that they are only worried about pregnancy or a sexually transmitted infection—the adolescent may say, "I will use birth control so I won't get involved in a pregnancy," and sexual intercourse becomes a permissible behavior. Parents should realize that talking with young people about birth control does not give them permission to become sexually involved but only helps them understand about reducing the risks of unwanted sexual outcomes. Certainly, if despite every effort the parents made, the young person did have sexual intercourse, most parents *would* want their child to protect him- or herself (unless such an action was against their religious beliefs). However, any discussion of reasons for postponing sexual involvement must go beyond such specific concerns to include values and expectations.

During adolescence the values held by young people undergo examination and change. This process is important because values are beliefs on which we are willing to act. Young people enter adolescence with the values they have accumulated during their childhood—most often, those conveyed to them by parents' words and actions. These have been accepted with little question because their parents believe in them. Nevertheless, in order to be able to act on them when faced with the variety of freedoms and challenges the world offers them, the adolescent must gain a different kind of "ownership" of those values. The adolescent must arrive at a point where the values are held because the adolescent personally believes in them, irrespective of whether or not the parent believes in them.

This process leaves the adolescent vulnerable. In order to get "ownership," the adolescent has to look at childhood values in light of his or her expanding ideas and experiences. The adolescent has to give examination to a bewildering variety of new values: those held by peers, those conveyed by the media, those illustrated by public and private adult behaviors. Adolescents need to temporarily reject some family values and "try on" some of the new values; they may even adopt behaviors that flow from these different values to test how the values fit.

For parents this can be a difficult time. It should be reassuring to parents to learn that research studies show that most adolescents eventually choose a set of values similar to those with which they were raised. Nevertheless, going through the process with an adolescent can be upsetting.

Adolescents become particularly vulnerable if they are trying to act on only marginally held beliefs that can easily be challenged or undermined. Parents may have tried to convey to their children that sexual relationships are serious and should be saved for only those relationships that embody major commitment—love with marriage, for example. It may have become increasingly difficult, however, for their adolescent to continue to believe that sex is for marriage and that marriage is "forever" with the divorce rate at least one out of three and sexual involvement among unmarried people more open and common.

The adolescent, therefore, may be finding it hard to continue to believe wholeheartedly in the value of love and marriage. This becomes a marginally held belief. The adolescent may become increasingly vulnerable to the message that sex is all right as long as you really love the person. This ties in with part of the old values and yet encompasses the new reality: "I love her and she loves me, and we're just doing what everyone else who loves each other does." Or: "It's not like I'm going to do it with just anyone. He's just about the most special person in the whole world to me. I'd die if he didn't care about me." Or: "It's O.K. We plan to get married someday."

Some parents may find themselves caught too. Perhaps they and their children attend a church that firmly teaches that sex should occur only within marriage; but the parents' values may have changed and they no longer believe it is absolutely necessary for everyone to wait until marriage before having sex. However, they still don't want their child to become sexually involved at a young age and they hope that eventually the young person's sexual partner will be someone he or she is thinking of marrying and/or will marry.

Explaining Values

When parents try to explain their values, they are not sure how to convey the complexity of their thoughts, so instead they give reasons: "You might get pregnant and mess up your whole life." Or: "You might cause a pregnancy and mess up your whole life." First, parents need to decide if it is the sexual behavior itself they most object to or the possible consequences of the sexual behavior. Second, they need to convey the full range of their beliefs to their adolescents since young people need an underlying rationale for their sexual behavior. And an important part of this rationale is the identification of the values underlying any recommendations or expectations the parents have. A parent might begin:

"I believe there should be much more to a sexual relationship than just having sex. I believe that there should be a real commitment to the other person. And commitment doesn't just mean standing by if something occurs, like a pregnancy; it means being responsible enough to not do anything in a relationship that could possibly be harmful to the other person. It means knowing that you're going to be in a relationship with that person a very long time and are willing to carry your share of responsibility for it.

"The school relationships you have are very important. You may feel like you want to know your boyfriend (girl friend) your whole life. However, you are growing and changing as a person and he (she) is too. To make the kind of commitment I believe should go along with a sexual relationship would not be a wise choice—it would really restrict you at a point when you need freedom and options. It is important for you to have the opportunity to develop to your fullest potential. That is why I believe you should be through school before you ever consider becoming sexually involved."

Discuss your values and beliefs with your children. Tell them why you hold those values and beliefs and how you feel you have carried them out and how they have worked for you: "The reason I believe this is because my own life experience has shown me that the important people in my life are the ones who have made a commitment to me."

If at times it has been difficult for you to stick to your beliefs, share that. If you did manage to stick to them, share that too. But share how you think you managed to carry it out even though it was difficult. If it was luck, say that; if it was through having certain friends, say that; if it was through your parents, say that. "When I was going with your father, I was much older than you. We were very tempted to have sex before our marriage. We didn't, however, and I think it was because we both wanted to have that first time be as special as we thought our relationship was." Or: "Actually, your father and I did not wait to have sex before we were married. However, I have often thought that if I had gotten pregnant and we'd had to get married sooner than we did, it might have changed the way we felt about each other, and our marriage might not have been as good. If I had known then that I might be risking that, I would have waited. But I just never thought about it at the time."

Conversations about values rather than lectures are a more important way to communicate what you want. Conversations are two-way, with room for exchange of ideas, feelings, and information. It is as important for teens to hear themselves voice their opinions as it is to hear you voice yours.

Sometimes, if the teen's opinions are so opposite to what the parent is conveying, it is difficult not to get angry or upset or worried, and attack the teen's ideas. Keep remembering: Initiating anything that cuts off communication reduces the opportunity for your adolescent to do further thinking and talking. The testing out of values and beliefs is a process. Counter-values and -ideas are an important part of that. After a lengthy discussion, however, if you get to a point where you think the conversation is doing little to reinforce the values you believe in, do not feel you have to withstand the challenge endlessly. Feel free to change the conversation by saying, "I have listened to what you said but I still firmly believe what I believe. I hope you'll think more about it. Let's talk about something else right now, since I think we've really exhausted this topic for a while."

The Importance of Expectations

Part of the guidance young people need comes from giving them clear behavioral expectations. It is important to adolescents that you not only clearly state your expectations but also give them choices about how to meet those expectations. "I really expect you to refrain from having sex until you're married. I think you can carry this out. You can avoid putting yourself in situations where you might be tempted to become sexually involved and also make it clear to those you date that that is something you will not do."

Name qualities that you think they can draw upon to carry out that expectation: "You are a pretty good judge of people. I respect the friends you've chosen and I know you wouldn't want to continue to date someone who continually tried to pressure you into doing something you didn't want to do. That would show he didn't respect you and was thinking more of himself than he was of you and your beliefs." Tell them what you think they should do if they feel they are having trouble in carrying it out: "I want you to feel free to talk to other people and get support there too. I know (our minister, your aunt, the counselors at a family planning clinic) would be glad to talk to you, if you needed others to discuss any problems you are having in waiting."

Point out any way that you can be helpful in helping the teen meet family expectations: "I just want you to know that if you ever feel you're having difficulty continuing to wait, you can talk with me. I understand that sometimes it does get difficult, and just sharing how difficult it is can help. Maybe there will be some things we can work out to help you."

Express strong disapproval if the teen fails to meet the expectations, but show your adolescent how he or she can make amends: "I'm disappointed you went over to your girlfriend's house when you knew her parents weren't home, after we agreed you wouldn't do that. The rest of this school semester I will expect to you to call me before you go anywhere other than where we agreed you could go." Allow the teen to feel the weight of the consequences of his or her misbehavior. "I don't know whether or not you would have gone all the way with your boyfriend if we hadn't come home, but finding you two in bed together indicates you are not yet ready for the full responsibility of a dating relationship. There will be no more evening dates until school is over this year unless either your father and I go with you as chaperones."

Because adolescence is a time when there is so much

room for growth and change, parents should have confidence that their teen will be able to learn from experiences and make increasingly wise decisions. In particular, making parental expectations clear to teens will go a long way toward helping them guide their sexual behaviors in a manner consistent with their personal safety and well-being.

10

Staying in Touch with Your Adolescent

As adolescents grow and change, it is important to keep in touch with what they are feeling and thinking. Although on one day they may seem quite content with a certain philosophy or attitude, within a few weeks this can be altered by internal changes that were occurring unnoticeably but surface with a difference.

Also, circumstances change. The girl who thought it would be easy to say no has now been dating someone she really cares about for five months and her feelings have grown and changed.

The world around adolescents changes. A prominent movie star is involved in an unwed pregnancy that is glamorized by the media. A politician is discredited for having an out-of-wedlock affair. A religious leader's sexual transgression is exposed. A new sexually transmitted disease emerges or the cure for an old one is found. These influence adolescent and adult thinking and may filter down to how the young person feels about previous beliefs.

Parents must work very hard to keep in touch with their adolescent. To do so, they must keep communicating and must include sexuality in that communication. They must keep talking, keep thinking, keep interacting. Often parents wish they could communicate better with their adolescent. They wish their adolescent would show more respect for their ideas and opinions. They often fear that the adolescent is tuning them out instead of talking with them.

Sometimes parents keep in touch in some areas but unconsciously neglect others. It is natural for parents to want to block out the fact that their teen might be having sexual feelings and beginning to find out more about how one person relates sexually to another. This is a very private area for most adults. Parents are often torn between wanting their own privacy respected in that area and wanting to make sure their adolescent is confident about how to respond to sexual overtures and sexual feelings.

Families work in different ways. While in one family it may be very easy for parents to discuss intimate sexual matters with their children, others may not be able to do so. Stay calm when you discuss a problem. Pick positive times to talk with your adolescent. Make a conscientious effort to do this. This is particularly important during troublesome times. Otherwise you will find that you and your adolescent seldom talk except when someone is upset or angry. Try to explain reasons for objecting to something your adolescent wants to do or has done.

Communication attempts that don't seem to work include:

- lecturing
- blaming
- being a martyr
- comparing
- making threats
- ordering
- name-calling

There are communication attempts that seem to work better. Adolescents may be willing to talk freely with a parent one month about sexuality and be reluctant to do so the next. Sometimes they withdraw until they are more secure in what they think and feel. It is important that parents value their progress toward adulthood and respect their changing opinions. Communicating during this period can be helped by:

- learning to listen. All adolescents need to feel that their ideas or concerns about sex are worth listening to.
- looking for natural opportunities to talk about sex with your teen. Use something you both see on television, a news item in the paper, a relative's pregnancy.
- showing respect for your adolescent's feelings and the force of his or her sexual feelings
- letting your teen express his or her feelings about sex freely. Don't be judgmental about what is said.
- trying to listen to and value your adolescent's opinion about sexual matters
- not interrupting your adolescent before he or she has finished talking
- sticking to the subject when you talk to your adolescent
- not talking to your adolescent as if he or she were younger than he or she really is
- keeping your mind on the subject when you are talking to your adolescent. Often parents find themselves thinking about other things, and this can be annoying to the young person.
- making clear the things you mean to say. Many times, parents say things they don't mean. If you do mean to say something, make it clear. Teens hate misinterpreting.
- asking to hear your adolescent's side of things and listening carefully for hidden feelings
- engaging in problem-solving together by (1) talking about the adolescent's feelings and needs; (2) talking about your own feelings and needs; (3) talking together

about various solutions; (4) making a mental list of all suggestions, regardless of apparent merit; (5) mutually discarding those that neither of you can accept; (6) choosing a remaining solution that is most acceptable to you both, or one that is acceptable to the adolescent and that you can live with; (7) avoiding over- or under-answering questions; (8) being interested in the things your adolescent does or is interested in; (9) not *assuming* your adolescent knows you love him or her instead of *showing* it.

Sometimes parents get discouraged. They feel their adolescent can't communicate, can't function very well at home, can't do well at school, can't do anything right. They are concerned that the adolescent may blunder in areas such as sexual involvement. However, parents must keep in mind that all adolescents have certain abilities. Some have better abilities than others, some have a wider range of abilities. It is important that parents have confidence in their adolescent's ability—the ability to grow and learn. They must believe that their child will learn to think things through, to manage difficult situations. Parents often need to be reminded that there are many people in the world who did not necessarily manage terribly well as adolescents, but who somehow made it through and have become successful adults. Managing sexuality is something adolescents can learn to do, and as they mature they will become more comfortable with and skilled at doing this.

What If I Can't Talk to My Child?

Try writing. "I know we've never talked about sex. It's kind of an embarrassing subject for me. However, I wanted to tell you for a long time how important I think it is for you to wait before you become sexually involved. I know a lot of kids are having sex. But there is only one you, and only you can make choices that are best for you." Sometimes just taking the first step and communicating in writing can make it easier to take the next step and try talking.

Try a proxy. Sometimes a relative will be willing to initiate the subject for you, either in your presence or in your absence. "Your mom's very worried because she has never been able to really talk to you about how she feels about sex. She's worried that because she hasn't, you might get involved sometime and she doesn't want that to happen to you until you're much older. So she asked if I would at least start a conversation with you on the subject and maybe later on she'll feel she can say the things she would like to."

Try calling on professional help. Ask your doctor to speak to your adolescent. Take your young person to an adolescent clinic or a clinic that has adolescent counselors and ask them to talk with your child. Such professionals often have the advantage of having worked with many young people and therefore the ability to anticipate their concerns and needs. They also can bring an objectivity to your adolescent's situation. But remember, it is important to realize that professionals cannot teach your teen your values or convey to your teen your expectations. They can only provide a source of information, communication, and support for your adolescent and the decisions the adolescent must make.

Try supporting community programs. Parents can also make sure the community offers programs about sexuality in which parents and children can participate. They can ask that church groups, schools, health agencies, youth clubs, or others sponsor such programs. Some of the programs can be aimed directly at parents. In the past, such programs have offered opportunities for sexual values and beliefs to be discussed; for parents to clarify their own sexual values; and then have given time for parents to learn better how to communicate such values and feelings to their child.

Some programs for parents offer them up-to-date information on sexuality, reproduction, sexually transmitted infections, and family planning, or sexual issues. Others' topics are more exploratory: Led by a trained discussion leader, they cover what participants know about masculinity and femininity and how they feel about it; what they admire in men and women; what they think about men and women and relationships in general. This knowledge is then related to the area of adolescent sexuality.

Some programs start out with a lecture and then break into small groups for discussion. Others may begin with a panel of professionals such as a pediatrician or specialist in adolescent medicine, a psychologist, a teacher who teaches sex education in the schools, etc. After their presentations and discussion, these professionals may engage in a question-and-answer or discussion session with the audience.

Other programs are designed to help parents assess themselves as sex educators of their children. They help parents examine their level of approachability. "Are you an askable parent?" is the theme of one of these. Parents are helped to explore their own attitudes toward sexuality. Then the program leaders review available materials to use with children of various ages.

Some programs rely on films or videos as their main program. They may have discussion sessions afterward in small groups or just ask for general audience feedback. One community agency has a video of a play for youth on making responsible decisions with respect to sexuality that it lends out to parents through the local P.T.A.s. Parents and children can watch in the comfort of their own home and structure their own discussions afterward.

Some community programs are designed especially to enhance parent–child communication. Such groups may start off by having parents and children write questions on unsigned cards that they hand in to the discussion leaders. Questions are used as the basis for a discussion. This allows both teens and parents to raise issues anonymously that really concern them.

Sometimes programs for enhancing parent–child communication are divided along sex lines. There may be one program for fathers and sons and another for mothers and daughters. During many of the programs the parents and children are together the majority of the time. Often toward the end of the program the parents meet as a separate group to discuss their feelings and concerns about continuing to discuss sexuality with the children. The children are at the same time grouped to review information and are encouraged toward future communications with their parents.

Other programs take a different approach to fostering parent–child communication. For example, one program requires that at least one parent register with the teen; however, the program staff divides participants into small discussion groups in which parents are never in the same group as their children. This program feels that teenagers are better able to give their opinions in front of adults who are not their parents and that parents are more willing to listen when the teen-agers speaking are not their own children.

Yet other programs are focused more on helping the young person gain information or improve skills in handling sexuality. The parent component is only an adjunct to the youth program. Parents are given information on what the young people are being taught so that they can reinforce the youth program. For example, this is what is done in the author's Emory/Grady Teen Services Program's "Postponing Sexual Involvement Program" for parents of young people.

Whatever parents choose to do, it is important that they do something. *Not* doing something may mean that they will first have to talk to their child about sexuality at a much more difficult time—when they find out their child is having sex, or find out their child is pregnant or has caused a pregnancy, or when they find out their child has an incurable sexually transmitted infection. It is never too early to begin talking with a child about sex. Parents must begin before it is too late.

Talking Can Make a Difference

In sum, young people *can* postpone sexual involvement. To do so, however, most often they need their parents to play an important role, the kind of role this book has discussed. Because of the possible negative outcomes of premature sexual involvement, when young people do wait, society benefits, parents benefit, but most of all young people benefit.

The parent who talks to their children is not only helping their children now, but is helping these children learn how to talk to the offspring they will eventually have. Don't let your children be the ones who say to their children:

> "My parents never talked to me about sex and about how to handle my growth and development in that area. I wish they just had had the courage to try. It would have helped me so much. It wouldn't have mattered if they weren't perfect at it. I needed someone. It should have been them."

After all, what are parents for?